MW01165635

Backyard Pearls

cultivating wisdom and joy
in everyday life

Carolyn A. Scarborough

Andy —
Mary — you
find wonderful pearls
and healing through
your book . !...
cheers
Carolyn

Copyright @ 2008 by Carolyn A. Scarborough

All rights reserved. This publication may not be reproduced, stored in a retrieval system, or transmitted in whole or in part, in any form or by any means, electronic, mechanical, photocopying, recording, or otherwise without the prior written consent of Carolyn A. Scarborough.

Visit the website at: www.backyardpearls.com

Copyediting by Alix Scarborough

Backyard Pearls: Cultivating Wisdom and Joy in Everyday Life

ISBN: 978-0-6151-7409-9

In memory of my mother, Helen Fandos Werner, who believed I could do anything and never let me forget it.

And in memory of my father, Dean Werner, my wise spiritual mentor and friend.

CONTENTS

ACKNOWLEDGMENTS

Where to begin? So many people have helped in so many ways, from an idea here to a hug there, that this book simply wouldn't have been birthed otherwise. Not only that, but they gave me the much greater gift of working with them. This project has been such a joyous clanking together of ideas, vision and companionship that it has added meaning and play to my own life. Never has "process" been such a delight.

Since these stories are inextricably entwined with my family's day-to-day lives, and I'd like to thank them first for simply being who they are so I'd have inspirational tales to tell.

Thanks to my supportive husband, Charley, for editing all the stories and tiptoeing in to offer just the right amount of praise and constructive criticism, a treacherous task at best. He's in the front row of my cheering section — in life, as well as book production — and I am in his, too.

My daughter Alix, a gifted poet and sharp copyeditor, combed through the manuscript weeding out errors. Despite late night work and last minute questions, she never complained, ever. She just opened her heart and generously gave.

Chloe, a humorist in writing and life, brought her great ideas and irrepressible sparkle to the project. She was always happy to offer opinions, as well as good-natured patience when I was writing and could not play cards.

Thanks to my sister, Liz Schneider, for her creative, meticulous photo editing and design that led to a beautiful cover capturing the spirit of the book. When my email blinged at 11 p.m., it was inevitably her with more tweaks and ideas.

My brother, Mike Werner, photographed and laid before me the perfect cover symbol — a sunflower, representing the radiance I believe is the essence of all of us. He was my technical go-to guy, 24/7, on both the book and website.

Thanks to Mele Agrella for her discerning photographic eye, Carla Smith for her last-minute editing, and Kimber Pflaum for guiding this book to the publisher.

Special thanks to Shelby Murphy, who blazed the trail with her Radiant Women columns and offered me a door into my own creative potential via these essays.

I appreciate all my friends and family who have been with me throughout this process, whether offering perspective for a story, technical help or simply encouraging words. These include Rilda, Charles, Mary Lou, Andrea, Robin, Sheila, Judy, Sandi, Maria, Eileen, Adrienne, Barb, Carla, Peggy, Gale, Jennifer, Kathie, Meeta, Saundra, Stacey, Michele, Valerie and the Austin WriterGrrls.

Finally, thanks to my readers, whose stories, comments and kudos always came at just the right time.

INTRODUCTION

backyard: a place in the middle of everyday life
pearl: something of great beauty and value, a miracle

When people hear the name of this book, they often tilt their head a little, like my dog does when he's confused. It doesn't neatly fit into any of the categories in their brain. And while it's not my desire to confound anyone, I'm also satisfied that it encourages people to slow down and ponder—to wake up to a different way of looking at things.

I believe that happiness isn't "out there." It's right in our own backyard, available at every moment. Yes, that includes the times when we're late for a meeting and the traffic light is stuck on red, or when the back door has been left open, yet again, and a swarm of flies are buzzing around the dishes that were left out.

In the grist of everyday life, pearls—moments of beauty, insight or joy—are always available. It simply takes paying attention to what's right around us and inside us. Before we know it, an "aha" is zinging our direction.

This book of essays isn't theoretical. It takes you right to the heart of everyday life, and then flips it over to illuminate a deeper meaning. After each column, you're given an opportunity to "Discover Your Own Pearls." If you're drawn to explore the topic further, you might read this section and ponder the questions provided, write out your thoughts or take other action steps.

These pieces were written as a series of biweekly newspaper columns. My daughters were 8 and 12 when the first column ran, and I continued writing for four years. Like all women, the topics here reflect the stage I was in at the time. Before children were my glamorous days as travel editor for international magazines. The stories in Backyard Pearls reflect my period of staying at home to raise the girls as I freelanced on the side. Today, I'm in yet another stage as a life coach, writer and mother of teenagers. All these stages have been equally phenomenal—as long as I resisted comparing one to another and simply settled into where I was in that moment.

My hope is that you can pick up this book and find inspiration and laughter any time you are in need of a pearl. Even more, I wish for you a life overflowing with your own pearls, a daily adventure in transforming the mundane to the miraculous... all in your own backyard.

Identity Pearls

LOSING MY IDENTITY

*"The Beatles exist apart from my Self. I am not really Beatle George.
Beatle George is like a suit or shirt that I once wore on occasion,
and until the end of my life people may see
that shirt and mistake it for me."*
— George Harrison

I t's only four basic words, but used in combination, they
have the power to transform outwardly confident women
to tongue-tied teenagers. I would know. Right after I quit
working, I tried avoiding these words in social situations,
but finally it happened. "So," a corporate lawyer said as we
speared Thai appetizers off a tray at a fundraising dinner,
"What do you do?"

I stumbled to voice an answer. I certainly wasn't going to
roll back the progress of feminism for the past 30 years and
call myself a "housewife." And I also didn't buy into modern,
politically-correct phrasing, such as, "I work, but not outside
the home." So I settled on the least objectionable label and said
I was a stay-at-home mother. Granted, this one too was
misleading — did it mean I was a mother at home, but once
out the door it was nothing but spiked heels and salsa parties
for me?

It wasn't always this way. At various points in my life, I
welcomed this persistent, four-word question. After all,
instead of the glazed looks and impatient sighs I got with the

stay-at-home response, I had received envious gazes, curious follow up questions, excitement! "Oh, I'm a travel writer with Southern Living magazine," I would say, trying to hide my slight air of braggadocio. Later, I wrapped myself in the feel-good cloak of being an international magazine editor, throwing out bits about editorial meetings in penthouse suites high above Barcelona, Spain.

But one day, in the midst of juggling three magazines, two daughters and one husband, not to mention a fading cast of friends, I noticed my life wasn't working. I had a gardener to appreciate the scent of gardenias in my back yard instead of me; an in-home cook to make egg-lemon soup instead of me; and a housekeeper to dust off my husband's whimsical sculptures instead of me. Where was I? Some women can manage all this — more power to them. But I had reached my limit and quit.

This isn't a statement about mothers who work and those who don't — this was the personal decision of one woman who knew what she needed. But if I was so happy with my decision, why was sharing it with the world so difficult? Why did I feel as if I had been bumped from first class to coach when it came to conversations? As if I needed an exciting tale to tell or an impressive title, rather than just being... me.

Eventually, a light came on. One of my epiphanies came with the words of Anne Morrow Lindbergh, who says in Gift from the Sea, "The shell in my hand is deserted. It once housed a whelk, a snail-like creature, and then temporarily, after the death of the first occupant, a little hermit crab, who has run away, leaving his tracks behind him like a delicate vine on the sand. He ran away, and left me his shell. It was once a protection to him."

Like these sea creatures, so many of us women erroneously believe we need that shell, that identity, to help protect us. To somehow make us "more." What we sometimes forget is that, whether whorled with sea colors or plain-Jane gray, singing star or soccer mom, even the prettiest shell is too heavy a burden. For our identities lie within the miraculous creatures inside.

Once I fully understood the freedom of dropping my shell, life deliciously opened up. Every time I didn't impress someone else, I impressed myself. Sure, I still struggle with the practical semantics of answering "the question" in a quick sentence. But I know that whatever words I utter in the moment are insubstantial, like froth on the sea. As for me, I'd rather be out wildly skittering on the beach without a hat...

Discover Your Own Pearls

What identities have you covered yourself with? Accountant, mother, artist, carpool driver, executive? What would happen if suddenly those identities were no longer there? What would be left? Who are you without your shell? If you don't find someone beautiful, glorious and worthwhile, look deeper...

CONFESSIONS OF A MOM WITH BAD SHOES

*"Never offend people with style when you can
offend them with substance."*
— Tony Brown

It all happened so fast. One minute she was striding into my closet, turquoise glasses glinting, and the next thing I knew half my clothes were in a bag headed for Goodwill.

Into the box went the nicked shoes. The worn out purses. The belts that fit me in college. The only thing she missed was my ratty old robe, which I had the good sense — or proper embarrassment — to hide before the wardrobe consultant arrived.

While some women hire wardrobe consultants to, say, find the perfect pair of shoes for the Armani gown they're wearing to the ball, my aspirations were much lower. What I wanted from her was simple — teach me to dress myself.

The jeans and sweater thing I've gotten down... almost. But with the rest, I'm clueless. Colors to wear for different seasons? Casual fabrics verses dressy? How to actually match a purse with clothes with shoes? The result is that I'm the person at a party wearing a Hawaiian dress when everyone else is in designer jeans. Or worse, with my sweater inside-out.

In my defense, part of my style blindness comes from a rather noble philosophy my mother repeated as I grew up. It's what's on the inside that counts, not the outside. I took it to heart. I spent a lifetime working on the inside, figuring anyone worth their salt wouldn't judge me by my bad shoes.

In fact, I still feel that way. But I've also found myself admiring the way other women seem to reflect who they are with clothing. They're comfortable in their second skins, be it Donna Karan or something off the rack at Target. They pamper their bodies with wool and soft cashmere.

On the other hand, I've always been the zebra trying to zip up ill-fitting elephant skin. More and more, I found myself in my closet, wringing my hands because I had no idea what to wear. Yet sending me to the mall to 'pick out a few things' is rather like opening a book for an illiterate and saying 'just read a few sentences.' It wasn't pretty.

So, when a friend said she had just met with Miranda the "Wardrobe MD," my interest was piqued. Imagine, I thought, becoming one of those women who just "throw something together" and look great. Or becoming a person for whom style is part of the everyday fabric of their lives, not something akin to a jackpot that happens periodically and unexpectedly.

So I called her. When she walked into my closet full of mismatched items and sale purchases, I was expecting a loud guffaw to erupt from its depths. Instead, she got busy tossing garments out the door for me to try on, and creating new outfits with what was salvageable.

Then, she gave me a shopping list of the "basics" I needed to buy. Like a foreigner learning a new language, I stumbled. Mules? Didn't they ride those in third world countries? Boots? Sure, I've worn them. Let's see, last pair was a red, rubber duo I wore during a snowstorm in first grade. A velvet jacket is the key item of the season? Well, shoot, and here I thought it was sweatpants.

But Miranda persevered. I learned about dressing to flatter my figure, "signature" colors and how good (read: expensive) handbags can elevate your whole wardrobe. We shopped for key pieces at places where they offer you drinks in curtained dressing rooms. And finally, we hauled my clothes to an alterations expert and had them fitted. You have a great figure, she encouraged, show it off!

And so, I'm slowly going from invisible to visible, frumpy to fanciful. I actually look through my daughter's style magazines and notice what other women wear. The other day I was invited to a party and the real test came. I stood square in my closet and challenged it. Admittedly, as I pulled my outfit together, I felt more like an amateur following a paint-by-numbers set then an artist with her palette. Yet, when I was finished, it worked.

I'm learning. I doubt I'll ever be a clothes horse, but I move through the world now with more ease and confidence. Nicer clothes help me celebrate my body — at just the age and weight it is today. Getting dressed is actually fun. But unlike makeover shows, my life hasn't been transformed. I think image consultant Brenda Kinsel sums it up best when she says, "Dressing well frees you to forget about your clothes... and concentrate on living."

So I'm living it up — in my cute black mules.

Discover Your Own Pearls

Are you comfortable in your clothes? Do they say what you want them to say, either on the job or when you're walking the dog? Do you feel they hold you back from anything, whether a promotion or confidence in new social situations? You deserve to be comfortable with yourself... inside and out.

THE NICE FLU

"Always being loving, gentle and good is deadly…"
— Susan Goldsmith Wooldridge

I can always tell when I'm coming down with the "nice" flu. The symptoms are unmistakable. I place a smile like a bumper sticker on my face and flash it to anyone who talks to me. I agree to attend a friend's Tupperware party when I really want to read my novel in the tub. At a restaurant, I sit at a table near the clanking, clattering kitchen rather than complaining.

I've been getting nice flus throughout my life, but I remember especially bad cases when I was growing up and tried keeping my world in harmony by pleasing everyone. When there was a fight, I mediated. When people were in bad moods, my Mary Sunshine always sailed in.

I wasn't even aware of the illness — until one day at church. I was standing in the refreshment area dipping into the sherbet punch bowl when a rotund Greek woman came up to us, pinched my cheek and said to my mother, "Oh, you must be so proud. Carolyn is such a nice girl!"

That was it. At 15, it was the ultimate insult. My mother beamed; I stewed. And I vowed to get rid of it, whatever this "nice" thing was.

It's not that I minded being nice, so much as I was annoyed that was the first adjective that came to mind to describe me. Nice? Nice isn't passionate or juicy or dripping with creativity. Nice is "pleasing and agreeable in nature." It's social niceties. It's tea parties with the Stepford wives.

I would have preferred being called remarkably gutsy, wickedly witty or even charmingly eccentric. But nice somehow implied that I had caught a bad case of the borings.

It wasn't until many years later that I heard something that struck a chord with me. Playwright Eve Ensler was chatting on TV and mentioned a similar four-letter word — good. She said, "We have to be very careful we don't grow up in a culture where there's good and evil and where these things are split, as if they all aren't in us at one time. My idea of good is this kind of messy, gooey, ambiguous, mysterious, delicious, complicated grief/sorrowful good. Not this perfect, flat, shut down, dead, pretending to be someone you're not good."

I finally understood that the reason nice bothered me was that, all too often, our idea of being nice is being the perfect person. We've categorized parts of ourselves as "bad" and thrown them out the door like so much old trash. When a piece of us isn't deemed "acceptable" — even if that judgment came from our 4th grade PE teacher or our high school jerk of a boyfriend, we shut down that part of us. But often those "messy" parts are just the ones we need to be fully ourselves, fully alive — a big, bodacious, bubbling pot of a little of this, a little of that. And that doesn't always look nice. As creativity consultant Julie Cameron says, "The true self is a disturbing character, healthy and occasionally anarchistic, who knows how to play, how to say no to others and 'yes' to itself."

Although I don't mind being called thoughtful, kind or compassionate, I'm happy to report I'm not called nice nearly as often as I used to be. I switch restaurant tables until I find one I like, I say "no" more often, and I proudly sport a button that says, "Say the thing that everyone is thinking." In fact, there may even be a few people who don't like me.

However, that pleasantest of flus still hits me periodically. When it does, I remember the words of poet Susan Goldsmith Wooldridge, who advises we be more like the coyote, a Native American symbol that is both naughty and heroic, true to its wild nature. "Coyote wants us to be free, to run and howl and play and lope and roll and eat our fill, at least sometimes," she says. After that, we can have tea and be very, very nice.

Discover Your Own Pearls

Are there times when you don't follow your desires because you don't want to rock the boat? What does it feel like to push down your needs? What payoff do you get from it? The respect of others? Harmony? And what, of yourself, do you lose in the process?

SMALL THINGS FORGOTTEN

"You never find yourself until you face the truth."
— Pearl Bailey

It started off all wrong. The road trips of my youth had all begun with high spirits and my humming "Born to be Wild" as I shot down the highway in my red sports car.

But I'm not a youth anymore. I'm a middle aged mom, and on this day I sputtered down the highway in my minivan, mainlining a java frappacino and listening to a local Mexican station crackle in and out of my radio.

I was plain exhausted after a week-long family vacation with little rest. My fantasy was a hot bath and 12 hours of sleep. But I had signed up to attend a conference for newspaper columnists in Dallas, so a few hours after our flight from Florida arrived home, I was off. Reluctantly.

Funny thing, though — ever notice how what you most resist often is what you most need?

As I drove, the road started working its magic. The giant swath of blue sky out my window teased of limitless possibility. With the scenery always changing, my mind melted into fluidity rather than staying stuck in rigid thought patterns. At the sight of a bale of hay, thoughts rose up of my cousin's old farm; passing by a Stuckey's sign, I recalled stops for pecan divinity as a kid. The further I moved from home, the more that cocoon that usually binds my days began to unwind.

It had been ages since I'd been to a professional

conference, unless you count moms huddled in the library for a PTA meeting. Before kids, I had been a full-time journalist, going to annual meetings in tropical places and hobnobbing with my peers. But it had been awhile and I was feeling, well, inadequate. What if someone looked at me and said "Hah, we see through that 'notepad in hand' disguise. You're just a mom!"

After checking into the hotel, it was decision time. The bathtub was luring me with its siren song of relaxation, one I doubted I'd emerge from all evening. Or, I could force myself out the door to meet the other attendees. I chose the latter, and spent the next few days shaking hands with increasing energy, as well as going to workshops on polishing writing, syndicating and speechmaking. I became fast friends with several writers, thrilled to talk "shop" with someone. But it wasn't until the end, as I was listening to an inspiring speech by New York columnist Pete Hamill, that it came floating back. A piece of Carolyn.

You know how it is. We become parents and, whether consciously or not, we drop some of who we are in order to fit "parent" into our title. Sometimes it's little things, like stopping the habit of a coffee and bagel at your favorite café. Or setting aside a penchant for dabbling in paints, or long solitary walks. Even your brain isn't yours alone, but is constantly inhabited by spouse and children. You willingly give them all this, if not more — dreams, whole careers. Years can pass. Then one day, a part of you rusting in some corner of the psyche comes back.

As I listened to the passion in Hamill's voice, it ignited my own. The part that rose up was my idealistic, journalistic identity before kids, my fervor for words and people. As I listened to him, I felt an inner shift. Tears threatened. Something essential had returned.

Driving home after the conference, the summer day stretching endless before me, I felt different. Still tired, but somehow satisfied. The radio's tunes seemed clearer, with less static. I was looking forward to getting back to my family; I had already gotten back to myself.

Discover Your Own Pearls

Sometimes forgotten pieces of yourself come floating up when you least expect them. Other times, you have to look more consciously. When one of those pieces comes up, what "story" do you tell yourself about why you're not doing it anymore? Is that story really the truth? Dig around, gently, and see what whispers to you...

ME AND MY SHADOW

*"Shadow work is about opening your heart and making peace with
your internal devils. It is about embracing your fears and weaknesses
and finding compassion for your humanity. Give yourself the gift of
your heart. As soon as you open your heart to yourself, you will open
your heart to all others."*
—Debbie Ford

It's ruined me forever. I used to be able to go to restaurants
and get annoyed at all the obnoxious people around me.
The fellow arguing loudly with his girlfriend on the cell
phone. The toddler banging her sippy-cup on the table for
attention. The waiter who serves drinks and then mysteriously
disappears for an hour. It's not that I enjoyed this, but at least I
could get the thrill of self-righteous indignation. After all,
you'd never catch ME doing any of this.

But now the thrill is over. I've found my shadow.

No, I don't mean that thing that trails after me on lazy
August afternoons. I mean the "shadow" theory, put forth by
psychologist Carl Jung and others, that whatever we are upset
by in others — their rudeness, their nagging, their greed — we
also have in ourselves. We just can't see it. The reason? We've
spent our lives putting together our ideal pictures of
ourselves, so what we don't like, we bury and often forget. Yet
it comes out anyway in ways we can't predict, like screaming
at the Starbucks clerk for putting too much milk in our latte.

The only way to find these qualities is to see what we strongly react to in others, and then do some searching to find that quality within us.

Jung is not the only one to have observed this. The Biblical equivalent is "Why do you see a speck in your neighbor's eye, but do not notice the log in your own eye?" Even simpler is what we chanted as kids — it takes one to know one.

Always up for a challenge, I decided to go on a hunt for my shadow and see what turned up. It didn't take long. The first "sighting" was with my daughter Alix. She was hurriedly trying to get out the door for school when she realized she couldn't find her school ID badge, which was essential that day as she needed it to pick up a library book. We searched and searched, and all the while I grew angrier at her carelessness, her inability to keep track of her things. We didn't find the ID, but as we headed out the door to school, I found something else: my shadow.

I realized that while I had been judging her, I had conveniently forgotten what I had done just the week before. I had lost my cell phone for several days before accidentally finding it on a chilly day in my coat pocket. Even worse, I had also lost my wedding ring for a day, absent-mindedly placing it on the barbecue pit while I pulled a few weeds.

Because of this discovery, on the drive to school I was able to feel compassion for her — and myself. "Sure feels scary to lose something important, doesn't it?" I asked. She agreed, and we talked about better ways of keeping track of things. Then we went on to talk about her concerns about school that day, which I was able to listen to because my head wasn't filled with anger and judgment.

Of course, once I "got it," sightings came fast and furious. When I was frustrated with my daughter Chloe for procrastinating on cleaning her room, I remembered the pile of laundry growing wrinkles in my own. When I avoided someone I judged as too "dull," I had to admit that I'm not always the most charismatic person in the room, either.

Once these qualities were dragged blinking into the light, I could then lovingly accept the imperfections. I could see where I needed more balance. I could move in the direction of my potential.

In Debbie Ford's book about the shadow, "The Dark Side of the Light Chasers," she says, "When we reclaim these disowned aspects of ourselves, we open the door to the universe within. When we make peace with ourselves, we spontaneously make peace with the world."

Of course, remembering to look for the shadow doesn't happen overnight. We forget, again and again. The other day I stopped by a café for a quick sandwich and pulled out my laptop to write. However, my concentration was broken because another woman was punching numbers in a calculator that beeped with every press of the button. I grew more and more annoyed. As I pondered confronting her, suddenly my watch alarm went off. I had no idea how to turn it off, so it kept going on and on until I buried it in my book bag to muffle it. Of course, it still beeped there — I just couldn't hear it.

And then I had to laugh. Without a shadow of a doubt, that message was loud and clear...

Discover Your Own Pearls

Think of three people who really get on your nerves, and three people who you really admire. Now write down what you perceive as the negative traits in the first group and the positives in the second. Look at your list. Without judging, open to the possibility that all of these aspects are a part of you, too.

MEASURING UP

"When you realize that you are indeed 'fearfully and wonderfully made,' you can get over worrying so much about your thighs and your crow's-feet and start bowling people over with your presence."
—Victoria Moran

She walked into the coffee shop swimsuit model thin. We hugged, then found an intimate corner where we could catch up on her life since she moved. My friend told me about her exciting new career, the beautiful house she and her husband had custom-built, and her children's triumphs in soccer and music.

I sipped my macchiato and listened, genuinely thrilled to hear about her successes. As the sun shifted on our table, she finally looked at me and asked The Question. The one that's spoken as casually as "Pass the butter" but which has the punch of "Are you worthy?" As she settled into her seat, she said, "So, what have you been up to?" Meaning, now it's your turn to impress me with your successes.

Suddenly I found myself scrambling for words. I frantically fished around in my memory for something interesting I could lay before her, something to prove that my past year hadn't been as boring as I feared it was. There was the trip to Hawaii! No wait, that was over a year ago. I was doing more freelance magazine work! But the most impressive names hadn't yet responded.

I simply had no yardstick tales to proffer. You know, the kind that measure your worth in our society. The kind that revolve around promotions (money measuring), new stuff (status measuring) and physical fitness (pounds and inches, preferably lost rather than gained, measuring). In that moment, I felt small. She was bringing gold to the table; all I had was a pocket full of rocks.

I remembered feeling something akin to this a few months after I had stopped doing magazine work full-time to be at home with the kids. I was hiking in the Arizona mountains with a friend and she asked what I'd been up to. In the past, there would be a tale I could relate with theatrical effect. Well, last week, I'd start, I was riding in a hot air balloon when it crash landed in a field and an irate farmer with a sawed off shotgun held us hostage there! But this time there was simply nothing to pull out of the everyday fabric of my life. The funny thing was, I was happier than I'd been in a long time — it's just that moments like lying in a hammock nursing a baby didn't make good conversational fodder. The important stuff couldn't be shaped into a good sound bite.

As my friend got up for another coffee, I continued to wonder if I'd actually accomplished anything lately. When I pulled the pen out to write my Christmas cards, what would I say? Nothing much to say this year, but have a happy holiday anyway?

That's when it started dawning on me how often we deceive ourselves into thinking our lives are "less than" if we don't have those easily measurable stories. When I listen deeply to my children day-in and day-out, isn't that accomplishing something? When I walk with my husband and we catch each other's hand and squeeze, grateful that there's so much love after so many years, isn't that accomplishing something?

What if I wrote my holiday cards and explained that, indeed, I had exciting news. I'd say that since last I wrote, I've learned to react to others with compassion more often than anger. That I've cut down the length of time I need to forgive people by half. And guess what? I still haven't lost that 10 pounds, but I'm much better at appreciating my body just the way it is.

I could go on to say that my kids haven't won a single trophy this year, but instead won something much bigger. My respect. One risked social ostracism by sticking up for a child who was being relentlessly teased at school; another wants her Christmas money donated to a fund for endangered animals.

What if when my friend came back with her latte, I said that my accomplishment this year was that I finally realized that the sleek body, the career, the big house and entertaining stories are all nice, but that I measure myself by who I am, not what I do.

And as for my Christmas cards? Well, if you get one and it's sparse this year, it's only because I'm achieving so much, I don't know where to begin...

Discover Your Own Pearls

How "successful" are you feeling right now? Have you looked lately at how you measure yourself, often without even thinking about it? Perhaps you put yourself down when you don't exercise regularly, or when a friend is making more money. Instead, measure yourself by how your inner qualities shine. Did you smile at the cashier today? Listen to a friend? Start making it a practice to observe, and appreciate, these often overlooked achievements.

MARRIED TO...
MY HUSBAND'S FAMILY

"Culture clash romances are always fun — especially for those of us who have a strong culture and the baggage of tradition to give us our very own 'in' take on the proceedings. We can laugh at the pain of it all from the outside."
—from review of *My Big Fat Greek Wedding*
by Andrew L. Urban

I heard the laughter clear in the other room. When I came in, my husband Charley was laughing so hard tears were running down his cheeks. Between outbursts, he pointed at the TV screen. Ah, another showing of "My Big Fat Greek Wedding" — in other words, our life.

Some people marry into families much like the ones they grew up in. Then, there are the rest of us. The ones who marry into families so different than our own that initial visits induce culture shock — despite the fact that they may have grown up in the same country as us.

One friend of mine comes from a large, outspoken Catholic clan and married into a reserved British family with only one child. Another's intellectual liberal group merged with a conservative Bible-belt clan. Rich marry poor; creative marry analytical.

My husband and I were each in for a surprise at the first holiday dinner with the other's relatives. I come from loud, expressive, Greek relatives; he from quiet, stoic, grounded kin.

He walked in the door and was assaulted with hugs and kisses on both cheeks. Then came the conversation — passionate discussions on schools, the Greek islands, and especially politics. Even my tiny yiayia jumped in, shaking her finger and babbling about those treacherous Turks. People talked with their hands as well as their mouths. The most divisive opinions came out because arguing was a form of friendly entertainment, not personal attack. Disputes were followed by homemade baklava and all was well.

Then I arrived at his parent's house, both wonderful people who grew up in rural West Texas. We sat down to dinner and it was, well, quiet. I actually experienced something called pauses between speakers. Sometimes, quite long pauses... long enough for me to watch a fly buzzing overhead, to review taxes in my head, to fidget with my restless hands that I usually "talk" with. The house could have been burning down and everyone would have calmly left without a fuss.

There was more talk when I visited his extended family in West Texas the first year we were married. The discussion revolved around the cows' health and bargains to be had at the local feed store. Despite the cold that year and the fact that we were in a small ranch house way out in the country, someone knocked on the door in the middle of Christmas dinner. My husband's granddaddy sauntered over and opened it. A man was at the door — evidently a long lost relative who had driven all the way from California in search of his kin.

Had the Greeks been there, the decibel levels would have skyrocketed with exclamation marks. Everyone would be hugging and long, dramatic stories would have followed. Instead, they just looked at the fellow like he came around every day, said to come on in and sit awhile, then went back to talking about hay.

At that dinner, and many others for years to come, my husband's family offered traditional fixin's — green bean casserole, turkey, Jello salad and corn bread stuffing. At the first Greek holiday gathering Charley attended, he tried some of the Greek stuffing (yamasi) and almost spit out his bite of chestnuts, raisins and ground beef. Imagine! So the next year he brought his childhood cornbread stuffing, and it went over so well he started bringing it every year.

Now that time has gone by — almost 20 years of marriage — we've both made adjustments. He can argue politics loudly with the best of them and loves Greek food. I've learned to mellow out in order to fit into the slower paced get-togethers with his family.

This past summer, our daughter Alix visited her nona and nono (Greek for godmother/godfather) in San Francisco for a week. The first night she was confronted with a meat she'd never seen before (a pork chop, as it ended up, which I haven't cooked in years), an energetic toddler and a bedroom where spiders popped in unannounced. Although she was having a great time, she told me it was taking time to get used to the different lifestyle.

Just wait, I thought with a smile, just wait...

Discover Your Own Pearls

What differences do you see between the family you grew up in and the one you married into? Are there any characteristics you feel resentful about or wish were different, or have you managed to observe and accept the differences in family lifestyles? What parts of your spouse's family do you enjoy? Are there any traditions from either family you'd like to incorporate into your life?

"EYE" WITNESS STORY

"Normal day, let me be aware of the treasure you are…Let me not pass you by in quest of some rare and perfect tomorrow. One day I shall dig my nails into the earth, or bury my face in my pillow, or stretch myself taut, or raise my hands to the sky and want, more than all the world, your return."
— Mary Jean Iron

While others were trying on clothes, I was trying on stories. "Oh this little thing," I said as I pointed to my swollen black eye. "It's nothing. The real bruises belong to that bear I fought off on our camping trip."

Too dramatic. I tried another.

"Black eye? Really? I guess that wild party got out of hand last night, heh, heh."

It was no use. No one would believe me. Guess I'd just have to stick with the truth when it came to explaining how I'd gotten this shiner. I also realized that, while younger people had exciting tales to tell in relating their various scrapes and broken bones, when you got to be my age, things changed. The stories weren't thrilling, just embarrassing.

Take my friend Mary, for instance. Her foot broke after she accidentally dropped a TV on it. Yulia twisted her ankle pulling it out of her shoe. Even my husband fell into this category. Nearly 20 years ago, when we were dating, his face got banged up from high speed bicycling. Recently, he once again had bandages on his face, only this time they came not from sports, but too much sun.

As for me, my glamorous mishap was tripping over a curb. Of course, it did happen after a grueling race had finished... between a bunch of wiener dogs. Yes, time for confessions. I had spent the day watching the dachshund races in Buda, Texas. While some people were training for triathlons, I was watching short brown dogs charge across a track as their owners frantically squeaked rubber toys to lure them to the finish line...

By Monday morning, my eye was swollen half shut and it looked like an overzealous Goth make-up artist had painted around it in purplish-black eye shadow. At home I didn't care. Getting out was a different matter. I'd seen the movies. I knew what people thought when you had a black eye, and it wasn't that you must have spent the day watching wiener dog races.

When I went to Target that morning, a woman I didn't even know reassuringly laid her arm on mine in the check-out line, looking at me like she knew just what kind of brute I had supposedly married. Others stared and said nothing. It soon became apparent that not only was I without an exciting story, but now I felt I needed to defend myself from an unspoken negative story.

I tried different tactics to avoid the discomfort that arose when I came in contact with others. Sometimes I'd wait to see if they'd talk first. If they didn't, the pressure became too much. I'd blurt out that I'd tripped over a sidewalk. No, wait, you can't trip over a sidewalk, I meant curb (now they're really questioning my story) after the wiener dog races (the extra details added to make it more believable). If some doubt still flickered in their eyes, I'd point down to my scraped knee as further proof that indeed, no one had socked me, otherwise my knee wouldn't be scraped, now would it? I might even nervously add that my husband was out of town when it happened.

I started wishing I'd done something less conspicuous — like drop a TV on my foot. When people see a foot in a cast, no one assumes your husband or boyfriend has had one too many to drink at the family barbecue and taken it out on you. More likely, they figure you've had a corn removed. I wanted a nice, boring story like that.

More and more, instead of wanting a dramatic story that showed how exciting my life was, I wanted the quiet story that showed how normal my life was. I wanted the story that was true. I have a loving marriage, relatively uneventful days I cherish, and every now and again I get wild and crazy... and head over to the wiener dog races.

Discover Your Own Pearls

What images do you try to present to others to convince them — or yourself — that your life is somehow different than it is? Do you make your life sound a tad more glamorous than it is to be admired, or more backbreaking to get pity? When you catch yourself doing this, compassionately ask yourself why. What are you getting by doing this... and what are you losing?

A TALE OF TWO LIVES

"Being a full-time mother is one of the highest salaried jobs...
since the payment is pure love."
— Mildred B. Vermont

It's a little known fact that before your children were born, you did not exist. I don't care if you were a globe-trotting celebrity or a Fortune 500 CEO. If you haven't done it lately, it didn't happen — at least not in your kids' eyes.

This recently became obvious to me. I'd gotten back into freelance magazine writing and had a phone interview scheduled with the general manager of a prestigious east coast sailing school. I told my daughters that I would be conducting an important phone interview and not to interrupt me.

Five minutes into the conversation, the younger one burst into the room hopping from foot to foot and rubbing under her arms like a monkey. I turned the other way, trying to remember what I had been saying. Then the other came in, persistently shaking a paper at me and silently mouthing something.

By the time I got off, I was livid. Just tell me, I spat, what was so important that you had to interrupt me? Ends up the first was wondering if she should start her shower yet (thus the body rubbing), the second defensively claimed all she wanted to do was use the copier. The one right next to me. The same one that loudly grunts and creaks as it copies because it's a zillion years old.

Two things became clear. First, in "child logic," it's not technically an interruption if they don't talk. Secondly, moms don't make important calls. Sure, mom gets on the phone to talk about leaky pipes with the plumber, or the latest book with her friend. But despite the fact that I spelled out that I was writing again for publications that pay more than a cheap dinner out, they didn't get it. Because, of course, I'd always been just mom. Carolyn the magazine editor/book author/travel writer never existed. They may have lots of imagination for playing, but not for visualizing me in a different role.

Some moms I know get quite testy about this. They regularly make comments like, "Yes, I know how to scramble an egg, I was once sous-chef at a famous restaurant" or "No, I haven't forgotten your allowance, just like I didn't forget to keep track of money when I supervised all those tellers at the bank."

Not that it sinks in, anyway.

So, fresh from the realization that my girls just didn't get my talents outside making pretty peanut butter and jelly sandwiches, I decided to flaunt them a bit. I happened to be working on my resume, and I asked my older daughter to edit it. Wow, I had no idea you'd published more than 300 articles, she said. Actually, 400, I replied, pointing at the exact spot on the page. Wow, she said again... then went in the kitchen for a sandwich.

Ironically, about the time they're old enough to get the concept of "I had a life before you were born," they're also in the stage of "Why is mom (or dad) so dumb, anyhow?" So, one cancels out the other. Granted, the fact that I never can remember in Blockbuster whether I'm picking up a CD, DVD or some other mix of letters doesn't help. But no amount of smarts will convince them.

To counter this, one friend of mine has actually started studying the finer points of chess strategy. When I asked her why, she said she wanted to be sure to squarely beat her 11-year-old daughter. That way, when her daughter starts commenting about how "dumb" mom is, she can remind her who's who in chess.

I was thinking about this the other day while getting into my car. I flipped open my phone and a message popped up on the "Welcome" screen. One of my daughters must have planted it there. In small digitized letters it said, "Hello my beautiful mommy. I love you."

That's when I saw myself through their eyes. They may not see the accolades I've won in my career, or how I cut a striking figure in my mini-skirt when I was younger. They may think I'm dumber than dust because I can't build a web page. But no matter. I'm the "beautiful mommy" they love — even when they're not showing it.

I may not have "existed" before they were born, but I'm larger than life now.

Discover Your Own Pearls

How fully do your kids see you? Do they know about past jobs or accomplishments? Do you feel that is old history and not relevant to who you are today, or is that a piece of the puzzle you feel it's important for them to see? If it isn't, let it go. If it is, go through old photo albums with them and orally fill in the background. Have them help you in updating a resume, or perhaps take them out for a special "date" and share a few stories...

POLISHING THE LOOKING GLASS

"... regard this body as a machine which, having been made by the hand of God, is incomparably better ordered than any machine that can be devised by man."
—Descartes

My teen daughter is appraising herself in the mirror with her new braces, and I know what she sees. Or, more to the point, what she doesn't. Because it's the same thing I didn't see when I looked in the mirror this morning. Perhaps you didn't, either?

Like the Cheshire cat, for her everything has disappeared except for her teeth. Her good grades, her compassionate nature, her power — all shrank beside that glare of metal.

It's something I understand almost too well. When I glanced in the looking glass this morning, I disappeared, too. All that was grinning back at me was my stomach, which I judged as too round, too large to be comfortably put in its place with a snap of a button.

I didn't "see" my feet, didn't appreciate the miles they had walked yesterday along a trail dripping with pink mimosa petals, let alone mundane marches from kitchen to mailbox. I didn't stare in wonder at my hands, tendons pumping as I kneaded dough and blossomed it into food. Nor did I appreciate the half moons of my hips, angling out far enough to carry babies and sacks of groceries.

What would happen, I wondered, if I started appreciating instead of judging? What if I sat and really looked at my wrists. Noticed how they bend forward and backwards, unlike Barbie dolls where the plastic arms connect to the hands in a permanent wave. What if I kept looking and really noticed the thin skin just below my wrist, the delicate, unruly forest of blonde hairs?

What if I saw my body the way my 10-year-old daughter Chloe sees hers? As we were driving the other day, I asked her what part of her body she liked the least. She had never thought about that before. Well, what do you like best, I persisted? She paused, then said she liked her arms and legs, because they had grown strong through gymnastics. She also liked her eyes. Aha, I thought, here comes the vanity. But no, she liked them because she could see small things with them, like street names on maps.

As I thought about it, I wondered what life would be like if we grew brave enough to stop focusing on the 2 percent of ourselves we judge as flawed — inside or out — and instead look more often at the 98 percent that is beautiful and capable? And then what if we went that extra step and accepted that 2 percent? Even loved it? After all, as Oscar Wilde says, "It's not the perfect, but the imperfect that is in need of our love."

Perhaps then I could look at my stomach and instead of fighting it I would revel at how it efficiently it processes food, how it curves sensually like women in a Reubens painting, how it's rounded like a fine porcelain bowl. I could see the white slip of a stretch mark tattooing my belly as a badge of courage.

Imagine if when we looked at ourselves in the mirror, the image reversed? Instead of imperfections, what if the only thing grinning back at us, Cheshire cat-style, was our brilliance? What if we looked in the mirror and saw the moon and the stars and the bright snap of sunflower within us?

As my daughter grimaces in the mirror, I walk up beside her. She still sees her braces. It is up to me, in this moment, to reflect back her inner beauty. I see it gleaming before me, just as I reach to see my own.

Discover Your Own Pearls

Every time you look in the mirror, right after that habitual critical eye has spat out its comments, add a positive comment about yourself. It can be different every time or just an affirmation that you start to use as instinctually as you pick out flaws. When you catch yourself saying "My nose is longer than Pinocchio's," then add "and I'm grateful that I have it to smell the roses in my backyard garden." At first it may seem like a silly reflex, but through time, as you put more emotion and emphasis on the latter part of your phrase, and you'll find yourself eventually skipping the first part.

I MARRIED
THE HOMECOMING KING

"...the burdensome practice of judging brings annoyance and
weariness. What benefit can be derived
from distinctions and separations?"
— Seng-ts'an

This is irony, I thought as I threw another handful of candy to the crowds from the parade convertible. Back in college, a homecoming parade wasn't exactly the place where I fit in. A bohemian café was more like it. Yet here I was, years later, tossing out Butterfingers along with everyone else in the "popular" group.

Driving through my husband's old college streets, my mind wandered back to my own days at a similar school. Back then, I carefully honed my reputation as an artsy rebel, dating the foreign students, protesting various causes, discussing the meaning of life in tiny cafés.

There was my crowd and the "other" group — the popular, athletic kids who joined fraternities and sororities and pulled sophomoric pranks in the cafeteria. They gathered in packs with a sort of easy confidence. I wanted nothing to do with them.

Then I went and married one.

The paradox is that I didn't marry just any of the popular group. I married THE one, at least by high school or college standards. I married the Homecoming King. Which is why on this cool fall day I was sitting in the back of an orange VW bug convertible, along with "the king" and our two enthusiastic girls, waving at the crowds.

My husband Charley's alma mater had called a few weeks earlier, asking if he could return during homecoming to crown the new king. It would be during the football game halftime, in front of thousands of people, with me by his side. Oh, and could the whole family be in a parade, they asked?

Gulp.

My husband's reaction was a mix of excitement at the chance to see his old friends, along with sheepishness about resurrecting a title and persona he had so long ago left behind. Our daughters were tickled. Be in a parade?! Get out of school early?! We're there! As for me, I was left in a swirl of thoughts about who I was in college and my role in the upcoming celebration. I felt a bit like a spy being asked to enter foreign territory — the world of the preps.

We left on Friday and were in the parade that night. The next night, I was introduced to the woman who had been the homecoming queen beside my husband all those years ago. I was secretly hoping for an overweight woman with bad hair. Instead, this "other" once upon a time — head of her sorority and go-getter — was still a size two or some small number I couldn't imagine. Her husband was dashing. But worst of all, she was nice.

Back in my school days, that hadn't occurred to me. Some of "those" kids could be… nice?

Then we all walked onto the football field, past the band students pulling out trombones, past the husky football players jogging out of the stadium, past the cheerleaders in their purple skirts. I felt very transparent. Would everyone notice that I had grabbed the wrong color boots? Or that I realized too late that my belt had no loops, so it was sticking out at a 40 degree angle? The queen seemed flawlessly put together, while I had scrambled up something that I wasn't sure had worked at all. After all, I'd been busy honing my views on the world, not my wardrobe. I hadn't prepared for this.

To avoid looking at the Jumbotron display with my face on it, I instead beamed straight ahead, into the faces of the new king and queen, a young, diaphanous couple with white teeth and idealistic smiles.

That's when it hit me. Despite everything, I was actually... enjoying myself. I was secretly thrilled to be in the limelight, proud to be beside my king, happy for this nervous, excited homecoming court surrounding us.

I never would have had this moment in my early twenties; I wouldn't have allowed it. Embracing the "other" would have threatened my self-view. Yet the more adamantly we hold on to an identity — prep, jock, working mom, democrat, responsible parent — the more we shut out others. Then, we start shutting out life. Simple as that. We either find a way to open our heart to everything, or we slowly close off and erect walls.

In this moment, I chose to open to all of it — from the grunting tuba to the disheveled photographer on the sidelines to... yes... the new queen adjusting her crown.

Discover Your Own Pearls

Who are the people you see as "other" in your life? The Democrats or Republicans? Stay-at-home or working moms? What about your next-door-neighbor? How has shutting off these individuals or groups made your life a little smaller? Has it added more anger or more tolerance to your life? What would choosing differently look like?

BACK HOME AGAIN

"I need time to go home and find out who I am."
— Alan Rickman

L ately, I've been searching for people with olive skin. I sniff the air when a whiff of garlic floats by; I pause to stare at the Greek letters atop a sorority house. I'm not weird. I'm just looking for something. Oddly enough, I think it's called "home."

Having moved around a lot in my life, "home" for me isn't a certain region. No, for me home is the place where it all began — the inside of a dark-haired woman's Greek belly. I was born into the welcoming shouts of "opa!" and kisses on both cheeks. Although I can't remember, I imagine people were commenting on my blonde hair with their expressive hands and loud voices.

Growing up, I recall gaggles of Greek cousins crammed around our yiayia's small kitchen table, passing around steaming pastitsio and avgolemono soup, a little extra oregano, please. With a shout of "Ella! Na horepsome!," yiayia would grab our hands and pull us to dance with her in the living room. And on Sunday mornings, it was quiet moments amidst a cloud of incense in the Greek orthodox church, listening to guttural chanting as men in long golden robes walked by.

All this seems a million miles away as I sit here in Texas, far away from my Greek relatives in Phoenix, St. Louis and

Albuquerque.

But we're back here because my husband has his version of home, too. When we were living in Arizona, amid my relatives, he never could get settled in just right. Maybe he was anxiously waiting to hear "y'all" instead of "yasou!" He finally realized that for him, home was a place with spring-fed pools, mesquite-dotted hills and family with deep Texas accents and even deeper roots. So three years ago we left Phoenix for Texas, for his home.

So often, we rush ahead without looking back at our cultural or geographic roots. We discard them like yesterday's worn out clothes. They're simply not convenient in our practical lifestyles. We move where the jobs are and become assimilated in the cultures of our neighborhood, our kids' schools, our careers. We forget.

Then one day it hits us. A familiar scent or sight and we're catapulted back in time. For me, that moment came last week. I was scrolling through my emails when a familiar name popped up. Papadimitriou. Ah, the long complicated roll of Greek names. A cousin I hadn't seen in years wrote to let me know that my 107-year-old great aunt Despo had died. There had been a lot of cousins at the funeral, he said, and he realized how out-of-touch we had all become. What about gathering some of our far flung relatives and starting a Google group and web site so we could communicate more?

Within days, relatives in Greece, Paris and the U.S. were reaching out to each other.

Newly inspired, a week later our family drove down to San Antonio for a Greek festival. Faded photos of Greek immigrants lined the walls of the church hall, and I explained to my daughters the story of how their great yiayia Stasa and papou George had come to this country. Then we went outside and clapped as folk dancers in black boots stomped across a stage, hazy with the smoke of grilling souvlaki. We ate kourambiethes cookies, laughing as the white powdered sugar dusted our clothes and faces. At the "plaka," the girls bought strings of worry beads and "Kiss Me I'm Greek" buttons.

Finally, my younger daughter looked at my husband and said, "You're lucky you married mommy. Now we all get to be Greek!"

That's exactly it, I thought. We all get to be Greek. Our roots are olive trees and Mediterranean seas. Sometimes we forget. Other times we remember, and get to go back home.

Discover Your Own Pearls

As a child, what was "home" for you? Was it an ethnic culture, a geographic region, or simply the feel of walking in the woods? What were the surroundings that made you feel safe and loved? If it's not in your life right now, how might you change that? It could be as simple as a visit to the seashore you loved as a child, or as deep as creating a family tree and reconnecting with the roots and traditions that are important to you. Perhaps you could return to a childhood faith. Just sit for a moment and see what comes up.

SENSITIVE SOULS AMONG US

*"Enjoy the little things, for one day you may look back and
realize they were the big things."*
— Robert Brault

I used to think I was simply persnickety. How else to
explain, for instance, my behavior in restaurants? When
the hostess leads me to a table, I know it won't last long.

Tables in dark areas won't do, but neither will a spot so
bright it makes my eyes water. If the party at the table next to
mine is loudly guffawing over college stories, I may take my
menu and move. And wobbly tables? No problem — I just
cram a few packets of sugar under the leg to fix it. It wasn't
until I found out about HSPs, or "Highly Sensitive People,"
that this and other behaviors made sense.

According to Elaine Aron, author of "The Highly Sensitive
Person," "Most people walk into a room and perhaps notice
the furniture, the people — that's about it. HSPs can be
instantly aware, whether they wish to be or not, of the mood,
the friendships and enmities, the freshness or staleness of the
air, the personality of the one who arranged the flowers."

Bingo.

In other words, we have a nervous system that's more
easily aroused than others. What other people naturally tune
out, we don't.

Take noise, for instance. When I'm especially tired, the
sound of my husband's electric toothbrush can sound like a

chainsaw. I get stressed when TVs blare in the background. And as for the glamorous idea of writing in coffee shops, forget it. Concentration is impossible with pop songs playing at what to an HSP are almost rock concert decibels.

Don't get the wrong idea. While being an HSP is challenging at times, it also makes life poignantly beautiful at others. Take going on a bike ride. My husband says that while he pedals, he watches the pavement ahead and takes in small gulps of his surroundings. It's pleasant.

Not me. I take in everything — the smell of barbecue wafting from a backyard, the interplay of light on the trees, the love I feel for my husband as I watch his calves pumping ahead of me. It's gloriously stimulating. The downside is that, in my reverie, I've been known to run into things — like other cyclists.

Aron says that HSPs are about 15-20 percent of the population. Our characteristics? Conversationally, we prefer deep over superficial; book groups rather than bunko groups. Often we're introverted, although I'm not overly so. She says we tend to be more right brained, conscientious and intuitive. We tune into other people's energy and emotional states, "reading" them in seconds. For instance, when my husband's in a bad mood, I often point that out to him (which doesn't help matters) before he notices it himself. Same with subtler states like consternation, mild elation or guarded optimism. It's a bit like being psychic without the crystal ball.

Parties are another place where we often react differently than other people. My daughter Chloe invited some friends for a roller skating get-together before school started. By the time we packed up the skates and left three hours later, it felt like I had staggered through World War III. The place was dark, strike one. The music was loud and the rink cooled only by a rickety fan, strike two. And in addition to managing the swarms of kids, I was trying to make small talk with the other adults. Strike three, I was out. I went home and fell asleep, exhausted.

I imagined anyone would react the same in that situation. But when I ran into a friend who was at the party the next day, she mentioned how much fun it was. Really, I asked, puzzled? Weren't you hot? No. Wasn't the music annoying? It was energizing, she said. Plus, she added, it was fun mixing with so many people.

That's when I really understood that, for better or worse, I'm wired a bit differently. On days when I want to go, go, go and can't because I need the buffer of down time between events, I wish I had a few more layers of thick skin. Or, when all the good tables are taken at a restaurant and I have to make do.

But on other days, when I stop to look at a cumulous cloud and am overwhelmed by its profound, immense beauty, I appreciate my sensitivity. Those are the days when the rich complexity of my inner life is as fragrant and enticing as my Greek grandmother's stews. I feel an electric buzz when my dog lays his velvety nose on my foot. Everything's charged.

We highly sensitive folks may miss some of life's more boisterous pleasures... but the simple ones are ours to savor.

Discover Your Own Pearls

Are you, or is anyone you know, a Highly Sensitive Person? How have you judged those qualities in the past? If you haven't embraced them, how might you show more kindness and understanding about those aspects of yourself — or another — in the future? Most of all, enjoy the sensitivities you do have and the strengths that come with them!

THE INVISIBLE WOMAN

"The sage holds to the inner-light,
and is not moved by the passing show."
— Lao Tzu

She didn't exactly walk into the room. Rather, she made an entrance, sweeping in with her plaid mini skirt — sheer almost up to her thighs — her feathered hat and large, clanking bracelets. My sister and I sat sipping our vanilla lattes in Borders' café as this woman and her gaggle of beret-topped friends whooshed over to the table next to ours. Heads turned. Snippets of their conversation spiked the quiet room, enticing tidbits like "hiking in Thailand," "experimental theater" and "sweat lodges."

Suddenly, I had the feeling again. The feeling various of my friends have secretly discussed. The feeling of being invisible.

It wasn't always like that. I used to be cool. I'd tell stories of the time I caught a plane to Haiti on a whim, unbeknownst to my family, and found myself in the middle of a voodoo ceremony and later almost sold into white slavery. With my long blonde ponytail on the side of my head, I went to New York one summer with my mother. I wore a wild, glittery belt and scrunchy capris, and as we passed actress Dyan Cannon on the street, I fancied that she gave me an admiring look. I was making my way in the world, trying a little of this and that as I explored my limits.

Yet here I was, more than 20 years later, inconspicuous in

my Levis and navy sweat shirt bought on a trip long ago. Instead of funky retro heels, my feet toasted in scuffed tennis shoes, worn from carrying sleeping children up the stairs and chasing runaway pets down the street. My unpolished nails had opened more packages of batteries than swept over a lover's chest. My hair was the two minute, blow-dried "natural" look rather than the smart styles out of "Vogue."

Even my car wasn't cool. When it's time for the valet to pull around the vehicles at black tie affairs, my husband and I wait in line as sports cars zip by, followed by the heave and gasp of my big green mini-van. Once, I interviewed race car driver Eddie Cheever Jr. for a magazine article, and he said I could drive a lap around the racetrack. Woo hoo — there I was going a good, oh, 50 miles-per-hour in my matronly machine.

So there I sat, blending into the blue topped tables, pondering where I had failed. And then I remembered the butterflies.

I had been reading on the front porch of my house a while back when I glanced over at the bushes and observed that one branch seemed almost, well, alive. I looked more closely and saw a few narrow bands of butterfly wings, their bodies still as they blended into the browns. As they sat in the slant of warm afternoon sun, I realized that while I barely noticed them because of camouflage, they still had the ability to notice everything else, from the breeze carrying the honeyed scent of white Lantana blossoms to the coarse leaves heavy after a rainfall. Just like me, they could see. See clearly. Even if they weren't always seen.

Behind my Mona Lisa smile, a warm comprehension came. Sometimes we forget that we make our way through this life not in order to be noticed, but in order to see from a deep, rich place. That interior place, I realized, had grown deeper and more beautiful through the years. Just as the butterfly does its simple daily task of pollinating, I do my daily rituals — chopping garlic for the lasagna, showing up at a recital, tucking away strands of hair and hurt feelings. It doesn't take the exotic and spectacular to grow. Just daily life, lived consciously, with love.

The girl who tested limits in high school is still there. But she's pushing the limits inward, rather than outward. She's journeying through patience instead of Patagonia, brightening her eyes with wisdom instead of mascara. She may not stand out in a crowd, but she's cool where it counts — on the inside.

Discover Your Own Pearls

Have you seen your definition of "cool" change over the years? What's cool to you now, both outwardly and — more importantly — inwardly? Are there any areas where you're focused more outwardly than you'd like to be? Finally, sit quietly for five minutes and acknowledge your inner beauty.

Mother of Pearls

WOMAN... INTERRUPTED

"The great thing is, if one can, to stop regarding all the unpleasant things as interruptions in one's 'own' or 'real' life. The truth is, of course, that what one regards as interruptions are precisely one's life."
— C. S. Lewis

The moment I sat down to write this column, it happened again. The doorbell rang, and out front stood a scruffy man wearing a soiled white undershirt.

"Roofin' company," he said.

"Roofing?" I said. "I didn't know you were coming today, nobody called."

"I know," he said bluntly. "Don't much like the phone. I'm here to fix the roof."

I have no idea why I was surprised. After all, it fit the pattern. In fact, I hadn't even seen the pattern until it came to me — at 3:14 a.m. — when my sleep was interrupted by a flailing arm from my husband's side of the bed. As I lay there half awake, I realized my life could be summed up in two words.

Woman... interrupted.

Take writing, for instance. Before children, I had uninterrupted flows of time to dream and scribble away. Now, it's become more like interval training — write, start the bath, write, help with homework, write, find matching socks, write, point the plumber to the leaky faucet.

And then there's phone conversation... interrupted. The phone rings. You pick it up. It's your long lost friend whom you haven't spoken to in ten years and she has big news. That's when the kid radar kicks in. They know, from three rooms away, when it's an important call. They'll drop everything just to come running in with something CRITICAL, something that needs attending to NOW. Like, how they should dress next year for Halloween?

Or, a sibling fight breaks out. If you're on a work related telephone call, the fight is guaranteed to be twice as loud. If there's a dog in the vicinity, being on the same radar kids are, it'll add to the noise. Same with UPS delivery men.

We all know bathroom time... interrupted. Before kids, this was a private function. But when mine were young, I couldn't even close the door. When they got older, the door closed and conversations happened through it, unless of course something desperately needed to be fixed, in which case said door opened again. If the phone rang (odds of which increase when you walk in the bathroom) you could hear, "No, she can't come to the phone, she's on the potty and she's been there a long time..."

Any parent of young children knows mealtime... interrupted. When Alix was an infant, we'd put her in a swing during mealtime, giving us approximately four minutes to snarf down our meal. Later, we braved trips to restaurants with colorful plastic glasses. Spousal conversation sputtered out in sound bites. "Guess what — I got a promotion!" "I'm thirsty." "Promotion?! When did..." "Oops, water spilled." "...that happen?" "My crayon broke." "Yesterday, my..."

And when was the last time you watched a grown up movie at home, beginning to end, in peace? (Yes, movie interruptus.) A two-hour movie at our house can take a week to watch. By the end, we've forgotten the beginning. Of course, 80 percent of the interruptions are food-related. So, theoretically, if you pile a mountain of munchies in front of the children as they watch their show in another room, you're safe.

But no. All that food, of course, means arguments over

who gets what food. Or whose food spilled, and now needs to be cleaned up. Or whose tummy hurts from eating too much food.

About the only time kids don't interrupt is when you're standing in their messy room, scratching your chin like perhaps a cleanup is in order. Then they're not only quiet, they flat out disappear.

So, why do we do it? We were once blissfully selfish, able to start and finish a complete thought, a complete romantic dinner for two, a complete novel... without interruption. We had career paths, not career detours. Why did we throw all that aside for a life of fits and starts, stop and go? A life where children — and roofers — appear without warning?

We do it because, ironically, we need a life with interruptions. Interruptions teach us to open our hearts to each other — even when we'd rather turn away. They bind us together in daily rhythms of give and take. They humanize us. And deep down, we long to be interrupted from our headlong rush through this short life.

Interrupted... from the day's horrible headlines by a tender, sweaty hug. From our loneliness by a spouse's flickering kiss. From our bad mood by a child wearing nothing but a pink boa and oversized cowboy boots.

Yes, we're interrupted by love... in all its messy glory.

Discover Your Own Pearls

Pay attention every time you're interrupted, whether it's by your child or a ringing phone. See what thoughts immediately come up. See how long it takes for you to "get back on track." Finally (since they're going to happen anyway), see if there's a way to embrace rather than resist your interruptions...

INVISIBLE THREADS

*"You never realize how much your mother loves you
'til you explore the attic and find every letter you ever sent her,
every finger painting, clay pot, bead necklace,
Easter chicken, cardboard Santa Claus, paper-lace
Mother's Day card and school report since day one."*
— Pam Brown

"This birthday party was so easy to pull together!" my husband exclaimed as he leaned back in his deck chair, sipping a Diet Coke by the pool in the shade of giant oak trees. My newly 10-year-old daughter was splashing with friends at a local pool, whizzing down the slide, completely carefree. I'm sure she thought planning this was easy, too. As did my teen daughter, preening in her new cherry-spotted bathing suit.

But I knew better.

They had all seen a stitch here and there, but none had seen the entire thread that had run through this event from beginning to end.

They didn't see how I infiltrated my daughter's class party at school, birthday invitations secretly tucked in my pocket, instructions tucked in my brain. Remember, my daughter had said, if Jimmy can't make it, then don't invite Chase, and if Peggy will come, then definitely give one to Sue.

My family didn't see the hours I spent with my daughter discussing the details and worrying about who should sit next to who in the car. Keeping in mind, of course, who had a crush on who. And they didn't see me in a mini-van full of screaming, sugar-riddled kids as I navigated the highway during rush hour, through the construction, as the tribal chant of "How much longer?" grew louder and louder.

What they see is the finished cloth — it is I who understand the work that went into it.

As moms, so much of what we do is invisible — from making sure the right brand of toothpaste is in the drawer to believing in our kids even when they don't. We ponder and stitch, smooth and straighten the threads that run through our children's days.

Sometimes these invisible threads are in the practical details... like backpacks. Backpacks are dumped out and scattered. It is mom who changes a bagful of chaos into signed permission slips, dates noted in an appointment book, drawings placed in a drawer for posterity and a report card hung on the fridge.

Often we weave days together with the thread of listening. When my husband comes home and lunch dishes are still out and dinner is arriving in a pizza box, he sees the mess. What he doesn't see is how I can be in the middle of a task, just within reach of that giddy moment when I can check something off my overly long to-do list, when one of our daughters will walk into the room. Their half asking, half shrinking look says they need to be heard. Now. So I reluctantly relinquish my dishrag, or skip the trip to the grocery store, and I listen. The minutes tick by. Nothing visible happens, yet everything happens. At least, everything important does.

That's how it goes through the day. Our invisible threads work on the essential pieces. The very energy of the house changes as we break out in a silly song when things are glum, become calm when tempers get unraveled. The thread anchors the cloth.

Of course, there are also days when the thread is stretched taut. When the fabric is crumpled and we feel more like ripping it than mending it. When we feel we can't even mend ourselves. At the end of one of those days, when we've collapsed from trying to accomplish too much and nurture too little, our child comes in and asks for more. Perhaps they need a nightmare dissolved within our arms, or a shadow chased out of their room.

We look up at them through eyes of fatigue and invisibly fasten our will, forcing ourselves to open our hearts yet again. As we hold them, lacing together arms and even strands of hair, we feel a quiet glow expanding out from our belly — the belly that first connected them to us with two feet of cord. That's when we realize this fragile thread that we weave through their lives doesn't just hold them together — it holds us together, too.

Discover Your Own Pearls

During the next couple of weeks, start becoming more aware of the invisible threads you weave. Notice every time you do something that holds a piece of the fabric of your family's lives together. Or, perhaps you work this magic more in the office or with a friend? Do you wish any of these threads were more visible to others? Even when no one sees them, do you take the time to see and acknowledge them in yourself?

ON-THE-MOM TRAINING

*"Any mother could perform the jobs of several
air-traffic controllers with ease."*
— Lisa Alther

I took a deep breath. It was time. I flung my mini-van into the fray, maneuvering around cones, jostling over speed bumps and avoiding collisions with massive Suburbans snorting by me. All rules fled as I attempted to drop my daughter in front of her school without injury to us, the van or the madly gesticulating crossing guard. Five minutes later the parking lot spat me out, but I emerged victorious.

After years of this hazardous practice, I figure whenever I start contemplating "re-entering the workforce," calls from headhunters will begin. Ma'am, they'll say, would you consider being a UPS driver? We need someone to quickly maneuver through traffic and deliver packages unharmed. I'll coyly ponder the proposition. Then I'll let them know I'll think about it. However, as someone sought after for her "on-the-mom" training, competition for my skills is fierce.

Imagine that. Nowadays, moms feel that staying at home with their kids makes them "rusty" and worry about what work they'll find later in life. Phooey, I say. With on-the-mom (or dad) training under your belt, the options are limitless.

Do you want to be a rancher? Once you've rounded up kids and herded them out the door, how hard can it be to corral a bunch of sheep that don't talk back or forget where they've put their shoes? And sheep certainly won't call from the range to say that they've forgotten their homework assignment.

Then there's always instruction manual writing, since we've mastered the skill of simplifying the complex. (The folks who are writing DVD player directions sure don't know how to do this.) When asked why the grass is green, I've seen few parents respond that it's because of a pigment called chlorophyll, used in the process of photosynthesis when in the presence of sunlight. We simplify, answer in a six-word sentence, and actually tell the truth most of the time.

Of course, due to exhaustion and the 100th "why" question in a row, we might fudge a little and say something like "It's green because the Jolly Green Giant was laughing so hard the color shook off him onto the grass." But then, that's just getting experience for our future job as a novelist.

Or what about politics? Half of a politician's strengths are already second nature to moms. We deflect hard questions almost without thinking about it ("Where do babies come from?" "Look, is that a deer running across the street!?"), we confuse them with language ("Why can't we go to the ice-cream store?" "Because in the eastern time zone, it's already closed.") and we "spin" ("What a colorful, uh, original piece of art that is.").

Yes, you say, but some jobs require an advanced degree. After all, I might like to become a psychotherapist. Excuse me? Are you saying we get no college credit for easing depression after a danceless school dance? For figuring out how to promote self-esteem when "all my friends hate me"? For test anxiety? We've sat composed while they cried, raged and vented before skipping out the door happily healed, leaving behind an exhausted puddle of a parent. We've dealt with schizophrenia (I stopped liking peas yesterday.), paranoia (That teacher detests me!) and mood swings wider than any on a playground.

This psychological acumen will also come in handy for corporate management, which seems easy compared to parenting. When asked to do something, employees are not likely to turn pale, grab their stomachs, and complain that if they do one more project they truly might die on the spot. Nor will they run into their office, slam the door and start hitting the desk.

So, when one day you notice an ad looking for a 911 operator who can calmly asses a situation and react quickly, send out your resume. When a professional mediator is wanted, say you have plenty of experience.

Or, when you hear a janitor is needed — someone used to heavy cleaning with little reward — you can say, um, perhaps you're a little too rusty for that job.

Discover Your Own Pearls

First find a mother — yourself, your wife, your own mother. Think about the skills they've honed through the years in this role, whether it's organizing, counseling, patience, etc. Then give that mom, even if it's you (especially if it's you!) a pat on the back and some words of appreciation.

OUR "PERFECT" MOTHERS

"How simple a thing it seems to me that to know ourselves
as we are, we must know our mothers names."
— Alice Walker

I was rushing through the drugstore when I spotted the sentiment on a Mother's Day bouquet of candy hearts. "Something sweet for someone sweet," it said. It conjured up images of June Cleaver in the kitchen cooking, chiding Beaver as he stole a sugar cookie from the cooling rack. I saw visions of the perfect Stepford wife laying out the dinner dishes. I saw icons of motherhood.

Then I saw my mother. A quite different image came to mind. It was of a fall day, back in my senior year of high school in Chicago. My sister and I were riding in the back of the car and we were looking for freight trains. Slow ones. When we spotted one, my mother pulled to the side of the road, as planned, and my sister and I jumped out and ran in the direction of the train. I jumped into the open car and my sister followed me. Then we waved and my mother waved back as the freight train slowly headed west.

This was the mother I knew.

Almost 10 years after her death, what comes to mind when I imagine her isn't the angelic stereotype. Helen may have made a thousand traditional meat loaf dishes with the correct side servings of vegetables and starch, yet I don't remember them. Instead, I think of when she got on a health food kick and decided that anything in a blender would be healthy. Wheat germ, eggs, ice-cream — they were all whirled on high to become "dinner."

Helen was like many women of that generation, staying home with the kids partially out of choice, but also because that's what society expected at the time. A wholehearted break with tradition wasn't in her nature, but small rebellions were. Why, for instance, watch a trial on TV when you could go downtown and see one live, she wondered? So she corralled me and my sister to watch one firsthand. What she didn't realize, until the judge singled us out in front of everyone and ordered us to leave, was that the trial involved "sensitive issues." Oops.

But when I was at the store, looking at the array of mother's day cards, I didn't see any for mothers with more spontaneity than sense. Or for those who bucked the norm. I saw quotes for mothers on pedestals, not those pedaling in their own direction.

While this holiday is a tradition, what it doesn't capture are the traditions invented by the scores of non-traditional mothers. Take the idea my mother came up with one year. She decided dogs should enjoy birthdays, too. So, she invited our miniature schnauzer to sit in a chair and join us for birthday cake at the table — an oddball ritual that we've enjoyed with many dogs and birthdays to this day.

It's easy to find cards extolling our mothers' love, selflessness and generosity. Those qualities are all wonderful, but sometimes we're so busy looking for them that we miss what's right in front of us. The places where the ideal image shatters. The faults, quirks and passions that make the women who created us not mothers, but humans. Delightfully different, yet easily flawed, humans.

While I remember my mother's overflowing love, her oddities are mine to treasure, too. Helen always cracked the window for "fresh air," even when it was 30 degrees out. She loved brand new library cards, Edward Hopper's haunting artwork and arguing politics. She drove us crazy correcting our pronunciation. And while she had conventional morals in many areas, she also had a habit of doing things other people wouldn't approve of... like dropping children off to catch freight trains.

Ah, the freight train. As it ended up, we rode all night before it lurched to a stop in the morning and we called mom for a ride home. In retrospect, it probably wasn't the wisest move. Certainly June Cleaver wouldn't have approved. Yet that boundary-pushing was what made her irrepressibly Helen — an imperfect human, a perfect mother.

Discover Your Own Pearls

If Hallmark offered to make a card just for YOUR mother, in a sentence or two, what would it say? Wacky but loveable? Hard working with a heart? How would she be portrayed in the cover art? Have fun imagining it and then, if you feel inspired, share your thoughts with your mother...

PROFESSIONAL MOM

"She never quite leaves her children at home,
even when she doesn't take them along."
— Margaret Culkin Banning

I thought I could pull it off. Like Wonder Woman. Instantly, I'd switch from "mom" to "polished professional" — a seamless transition in which I'd toss aside my stretched out sweaters and practical shoes and instead wear chic skirts and take urgent calls, my expertise saving the day.

That illusion didn't last long.

When I accepted a six-week, full-time project, it hadn't occurred to me that my closet was full of outfits perfect for fossil hunting with kids along Shoal Creek or chatting with other "stay at home" moms at Starbucks, but not the outfits required for video shoots. Of course, this idea didn't come to me until I was frantically tearing through my closet trying to find something to wear, my hair flying every which way with each sweater yanked on and later thrown aside.

Finally dressed, I was driving to the shoot when I realized one of my earrings had disappeared during my Wonder Woman clothes changing. So I pulled off the other earring and put it in my lap, only to discover a big stain that I had somehow missed before.

Great. I wasn't Wonder Woman, I was Lucy Ricardo... on a bad day.

But that still didn't deter me. I was convinced I could

return to my pre-children days, when I was a bright-eyed career girl with cool clothes, ambition and exemplary performance. Always the professional, right down to my answering machine message.

By the next day, I was prepared — or so I thought. I had located my tape recorder behind a Barbie computer game and dredged work files from amidst summer camp literature. The night before I had carefully chosen an outfit and now was feeling rather smug... until I arrived at the television station and it started raining. Torrentially. As I sat in the car, I wiped the fog off the window and spotted another woman walking through the parking lot in a stylish raincoat with matching umbrella. That's when I realized that my umbrella — a hot pink number I share with my 8-year-old daughter — was currently nestled in her backpack at school. I searched the car for a substitute. Moments later I too was running through the lot — with a large silver freezer bag I used for grocery visits flapping over my head.

Once in the meeting, it didn't get much better. Everyone else had matching putty colored legal pads; I had a brightly colored spiral with hearts on it that I had snagged from the Walgreen's bargain bin. To make matters worse, I opened it to discover my daughter's stick figures cart wheeling on the first page, swirling doodles on the second page, a birthday guest list scrawled on the third...

That's when I thought of confetti eggs. You know, the kind that someone breaks over you on Easter, and those colorful bits of paper and sparkle settle into your hair, stick to the sweat of your skin, tangle in the fabric of your fuzzy sweater? Then, even after you think you've wiped away every last bit of the confetti, you walk into a store and people give you indulgent smiles and sidelong glances as they spot those wayward sparkles.

I realized that, try as I might to shake off the tell-tale signs of being a mom, they clung to me like confetti.

I thought I had wanted to transform myself into a smooth professional, but that messy, magical mom part of me can't be dusted off so easily. Nor would I want it to be.

It is our adventure with children that adds the extra depth, patience and twinkle we pack in our briefcase in the morning. The Hershey kisses and sweet-smelling hugs we steal at the school Valentine's party add a glow that lasts through the work day. The rigid perfectionism of our youth deepens into the flexibility and acceptance of our maturity.

I still change into my professional costume, even though some days the Wonder Woman cape is a bit wrinkled and untidy. As I sit in a meeting, I smile to myself as I glance down at the nick I got while shaving, now protected with a neon pink band aid my daughter lovingly put on. Some confetti you never want to shake off...

Discover Your Own Pearls

What "brands" you as a mother that you can appreciate, rather than resist? Perhaps it's the dinged mini-van with the school stickers on back? Or the wardrobe that consists of "washable" fabrics? Maybe it's the entry hall where kid droppings, such as pencils or stray beads, never completely disappear? Embrace it all.

TO GRANDMOTHER'S HOUSE WE GO

*"Grandparents somehow sprinkle a sense of
stardust over grandchildren."*
— Alex Haley

Any passerby would say it was just a small, 1930's house near downtown St. Louis with a rather forgettable front yard. I don't imagine it sold for very much, and when I visited it years later, I saw it had deteriorated further. But as I walked down the side alley beside its brick façade, I smiled because I knew what the other passersby didn't — that this had been a magical house.

My yiayia (Greek word for grandmother) and papou (grandfather) used to live there. Having never been a grandparent, I don't know if a special sack of magic dust is bestowed upon you when grandchildren are born, but I know that every inch of that house had magic, from the creaky stairs that led to the attic to the glassed-in back porch where surprise birthday parties appeared out of nowhere.

Funny thing, though. I've discovered that very same magic at another house, 30 years later — through the eyes of my own children. When they visit their grandparents' (called "granny and dado") home in Round Rock, the house is transformed. Whereas some people might see a cramped spare bedroom, my daughter sees a boundless paradise. Especially the closet. She opens the doors to a cornucopia of colored paper, stickers, stampers, and objects that can't even be categorized — an endlessly flowing treasure trove glimmering with creative possibility.

Another bedroom is really a time travel machine. Old quilts spill out of a trunk. Souvenirs from long ago events whisper their stories. Black and white images of great-grandparents sit on the antique dresser, beckoning with mysterious smiles.

I used to wish we had a summer home. Then the whole extended family could make memories in some far off locale, from a cottage on Lake Tahoe to a sturdy log cabin in the woods. Or, perhaps the girls' grandparents could live in, say, a beach house in California so visits would be momentous. What eluded me was that a grandparent's house is special, no matter where it is, no matter what the size. As we sit on the porch swing in the enclosed patio at Granny and Dado's house, the clicking of mancala beads mixing with birdsong, the flash of orange goldfish in the pond just outside, the scent of warm biscuits wafting by, I can't imagine anything more perfect — even on the beach. Take a simple place, imbue it with love, and it transforms. When all is right with the world, location doesn't matter.

When the girls return from Granny and Dado's house, there's always a bit of a letdown. Our home just doesn't measure up. I think it's like hearing a favorite song. When you hear it occasionally, you appreciate it more each time. But play it over and over, day in and day out, and it becomes mundane. Our house is the Top 40 hits list.

At a grandparent's house, kids are treated like royalty. Regular rules don't apply. Like silly putty, time and surroundings stretch in non-routine ways. Alarm clocks are shut off. Sleep comes at midnight and ends the next day with the sizzle of grilled cheese sandwiches for lunch. Beds change from practical furnishings to the scene of undercover giggling, or a cozy spot to hear about the times Dado sent balls whizzing over the roof of his one-room schoolhouse in west Texas. And while the voices at our house are likely to be saying, "Have you finished your homework yet?" at Granny's house you're more likely to hear, "You want another cookie? Why sure, have three!"

My yiayia and papou are long gone, but I can still retrace in my memory every crack on their worn linoleum steps, the breeze through the attic, the Greek cookies hidden in the antique hutch. We'd sneak those cookies upstairs at night, leaving behind a white trail of powered sugar.

Maybe that was the magic dust! We certainly ate enough cookies to coat the place. Or maybe it was just the unconditional love sifted into that sugar, a love so powerful it not only filled the rooms, but traveled through time to where it reaches me today.

As I look towards the future, I imagine my own grandchildren on the patio where I write these words, turning the wind chimes' music into magical fairy song, the yard into an enchanted forest. And I smile.

Discover Your Own Pearls

If you haven't experienced a "magical" house, either from your own childhood or through the eyes of your children, imagine what it might look like. What secret places would you have in there? What flowers would grow wild in the back yard? What loving presence would live in the house? Take a few minutes and imagine it all — then, go back and "visit" whenever you want to.

A MIDSUMMER'S HECTIC DAY

*"If you don't like something, change it; if you can't change it,
change the way you think about it."*
— Mary Engelbreit

There's no escaping. Everywhere I go, they go. I steal
away to my home office to write, and then I hear the
scrape of ladders moving, a thud, and before long
white, hairy legs are climbing the rungs outside my
window. A moment later, someone's wailing about biscuits
with gravy from the paint-flecked radio the house painters
have plugged in outside. I flee to my bedroom. Scrape, thud,
and Willie is singing about being on the road again.

Like a hunted fox, I flee from room to room, laptop in
hand. If it's not the painters, it's the rest of the posse. I reach a
stretch of open space and rest, but there I'm an easy target for
my daughters, home for summer vacation. Is there anything
to eat, they query. Do you know where my jean shorts are? I
dropped them in the dirty clothes bin, like, two weeks ago,
they complain…

Finding time for laundry. What an interesting concept, I
think as I sidestep the dog expectantly trotting towards me
with a ball in his mouth.

This wasn't exactly how I had visualized my summer. I'd
planned to not only catch up on writing projects, but also
organize closets and drawers with the girls. There would be
swaths of empty time where everyone could lounge around

and read. Our family photos, boxed and waiting to be put in albums for years, would finally be admired and placed in books.

But none of that had happened. In fact, for the past week, I haven't even found a spot of quiet time to write, and my deadlines are all coming up.

Balancing the laptop on my knees in the den, I try once again. Scrape, thud, and suddenly I hear the painters' hoarse little radio outside boast that there's never been a better time to buy an Evergreen RV, so act now!

Concentrate, I tell myself.

My daughter walks by, her arm swinging like an elephant, a small backpack dangling from it. The elephant stops, looks over at me, and wants to know if I'd like to see the contents of her backpack. All 112 carefully chosen items. No, I'm trying to write, I answer back.

Things get quieter. Ahhh, I can get something done, I think. Then a niggling thought. I open my appointment book and notice my older daughter has an orthodontist appointment — in 10 minutes. My laptop slams shut, I prod my teenager's slack body from the couch and we're out the door, slipping on the painter's plastic covering the porch steps. There goes another hour. Another handful of paragraphs. Another load of clothes.

As I get home, the words "I've got a Humpty Dumpty heart, someone broke it apart" come twanging at me across the yard. Inside, the dog nudges the bell on the door to go out. The guinea pigs squeak for more food. I know that at any point I could explode like Mount St. Helens. Small eruptions have been puffing up all day. My husband calls — he left his sport coat at home, could I be so good as to drop it off for him?

That's it. I finally give up. I let go of my visions of order and peace. Of getting my projects done. Of clean t-shirts. I throw my agenda into the tidal wave of life that flows through my house.

The fact of the matter is, my resisting this life is as pointless as trying to stop the ocean. Life will follow me wherever I go, from room to room, moment to moment.

What needs to get done will get done, I realize, but on life's timetable, not mine. It's time to drop the struggle.

So, I put down my laptop and ruffle my daughter's damp hair. I inhale the scent of baby shampoo, noticing how her blonde tendrils curl up on the end. When the words "Up against the wall, redneck mother" come floating by, I freeze in frustration for an instant. Then I release a deep breath, take my daughter's hand, and we begin to move a few steps in time with the music.

Discover Your Own Pearls

Summer has a different pace from the rest of the year. Sometimes it's slower, sometimes faster, more hectic, with kids at home and schedules tossed to the wind. What is usually the pace of your summer? Do you feel relaxed or rushed? If it's the latter, look and see where you're fighting against something that can't be changed. How can you relax into it, change your perspective by doing nothing more than accepting it? Where can you drop things that don't "have" to be done? You may not be able to change events, but giving up the struggle goes a long way towards finding your peace...

THE MOM CAR

"A man's got to do what a man's got to do.
A woman must do what he can't."
— Rhonda Hansome

"Do you have any tissues in this car?" my husband sniffed as we drove past yet another field of ragweed. Excuse me? Tissues? Asking me if there were tissues in the car was like asking if there was butter in the fridge, or toothpaste in the bathroom. It seemed so obvious it needed almost no answer. Of course there were tissues — we were in the "mom car."

A "dad car" is different. Last time I was in his truck and needed tissues, I was handed a wad of Arby's napkins — I guess that's what passes for tissues when you're a guy. But a mom car is stocked. It's a rolling first-aid station, coffee shop and counseling center. A dad car is, well, a car. Neat, clean, sometimes even cool, but not the stuff of drama. There's very little "stuff" at all, in fact, because that's mom's specialty.

For instance, my car has a whole category of "just in case" stuff. I have a collapsible captain's chair, sun block and bug spray, in case we see a park with mossy oaks and creeks too tempting to pass up. Cough drops, although they're usually not needed until we're in a movie and the van is parked two miles away. And eyeglass cleaner, just in case I spot a smudge on my daughter's specs while driving to school.

There are also things that propagate in my van during the

night, since they inexplicably multiply every time I open the door: incorrectly folded maps, expired coupons and old receipts, often unreadable because something has spilled on them and washed out the ink. Often it's something sticky. A mom car just isn't official until there's something sticky, somewhere. Hopefully, not on the driver's seat.

You don't even have to look inside to spot a mom car — it's obvious from the road. A mom car is often bigger and boxier, a womb on wheels, big enough to carry everything from straight-A boasting to weepy tales of locker room betrayals. A dad car is less emotional. Often, that's because dads are busy listening to music coming through the state-of-the-art sound system in their vehicles. We get the tinny stereos. After all, one doesn't need high definition to hear "The Sound of Music" for the 11th time.

Bumper stickers are another giveaway. When my daughter was "Student of the Month" and wanted that fact publicly proclaimed on my car, I couldn't deny her. I sacrifice everything else for her, why not my car? My husband loves her equally, but the car! Gasp! He just couldn't work up the nerve to do it.

If a mom car breaks down, no worries. There's often enough food in there for a week, as well as antibacterial wipes and enlightening reading such as Captain Underpants. If we're stranded at night, there are whimsical paper glasses that, when put over your eyes, turn oncoming car headlights into rainbow colors. Calamity turns to entertainment. The only thing you won't find is something to actually fix the car, like jumper cables. Those, you'd find in a "dad car."

Dad cars are repositories of fix-it stuff, from bungee cords to tiny gadgets that are unidentifiable to the average mom. Whereas we prepare for kid challenges, they prepare for car challenges. Why else would there be a flashlight the size of a bowling ball in my husband's car? Somehow, I don't think it's just in case he's driving at night and wants to take a romantic hike by the lake.

For the most part, though, a dad car is obvious not by what's in there, but what's not. There are no hot pink sandals on the floor. No strand of tinsel that got caught on a child's shoe and nested in the car until the following Christmas. No gymnastics "You're Great!" sticker in the back seat. Their glove compartment contains nothing but an owner's manual.

So, would I swap my grubby, lived in mom car for the pristine, groovy dad car with the booming stereo? No way. If I did that, I'd also have to swap the memory of a gaggle of teenagers passing around a hairbrush and singing the silly coconut song on the way to their first school dance. Or a bunch of creek waders baptized in Bull Creek, piling into the van with muddy feet and tales of frogs, waterfalls and dogs retrieving rocks.

The whole theater of Greek comedy and tragedy plays out right here, inside the green metal cocoon of my mini-van. Some days the scenes crack us all up and other drivers stare. Other times the stories are messy and punctuated with broken sobs. But that's okay. In a mom car, there are plenty of tissues to go around.

Discover Your Own Pearls

Look through the items in your car with a scientist's eye. What's in there, and what does it say about you? What about your spouses' car? Have fun and see if there's anything you can learn about yourself along the way.

Everyday Pearls

THE CLATTER OF CLUTTER

"Out of clutter, find simplicity. From discord, find harmony.
In the middle of difficulty, lies opportunity."
— Albert Einstein

"I'm just going to get more wrinkled the more I lie around here," the voice said. For a moment I dreamed I was tanning in Acapulco, and the voice was that of my husband as we lay there, sipping pink drinks and feeling the curl of waves licking our toes. But this wasn't a soothing voice. It had an edge of accusation to it. As I looked around, I disappointedly acknowledged that the only sand was in my Zen garden, and that was buried so deeply under a pile of folders I couldn't see it anyway.

No, the voice wasn't that of my husband; it was coming from the direction of the clothes piled up in a corner of my bedroom. It continued, "Just because you've neatly laid us here doesn't mean we're invisible..."

I sighed. It seems no matter what I do, clutter chases me, a beast untidily dressed in wrinkled clothes and trailing paper clips, trading cards, slinkys and rubber bands in its wake. As soon as I've shooed it from one room, it appears in a hall closet, or a kitchen counter, or the foot of the children's beds.

We even try to stuff it in drawers. Just as birds build their nests with bits of string and hair, so, too, are "junk" drawers lined with broken bits of things — screws, stale gum, used Chapstick and those Girl Scout patches that were never sewn on but never thrown out, either. Clutter is a weird amalgam of things. Some don't have a home, others just never make it there. So, the trading card sits with the pencils, each warily uncomfortable, neither one at ease.

No one's proud of their mess — if we were, we'd put it on the mantle under a spotlight and show our guests the "newest" pile every week. Instead, we guiltily try to obscure it. But, just as you can't really hide those 10 extra pounds under a poofy dress, you can't really hide clutter no matter how crafty you are. You still know it's there. And that's the problem.

Clutter can make you feel lousy. Every pile admonishes you, saps your energy. On some days, just looking at it feels overwhelming and you'd retreat to your bed if you could, but you can't — it's spotted with paperwork and books.

Sometimes, though, the idea of no clutter is a scary thought. It's an empty space. We hold onto clutter because we think it will keep us safe, like a homeless person spreading papers around them on a chilly night to keep warm. It's an emotional barrier, a comfort zone. But any wall that keeps us contained also keeps us from reaching out, from fully tapping into the energy that awaits us when we free rooms, drawers and mental space from the shackles of too much stuff.

Despite the grumbling, after my daughter Chloe picks up her room, she's energized by the clean slate of wall and shelf, her mind fertile with imaginative games. The space is so alluring she often throws a party. Everyone's invited, and with markers in hand we draw on her wall to wall whiteboard, listen to music from the pink boom box and down Dixie cups full of Kool-Aid.

As a child my yiayia (grandmother) would come in my room, yell "junks!" in her heavy Greek accent and the offending items would disappear. We'd turn pale if we found her in our room with a box at her side. But admittedly I always enjoyed the clean room afterwards, and when the grandkids went to her house, we were able to explore all the secret closets — where we could play because they were clean — and the mysterious, shadowy world of the basement. Her clutter-free zone unleashed tremendous creative energy in us.

And that's really the point. Clutter isn't just physical. It's mental. Clutter crowds our minds just as it does our homes. We can't be open for something new and wonderful to enter our lives when our minds are stuffed with the past. Yet that's exactly what clutter encourages. When we release clutter, we capture clarity. We create calm, not calamity.

William Morris, father of the British Arts and Crafts movement, once said "Have nothing in your houses that you do not know to be useful or believe to be beautiful." Useful and beautiful. I like that. It's calming to look at beauty, at the light bouncing off your favorite vase accented with a single rose, at clean lines. Even if my day is hectic, my home can be a truly rejuvenating sanctuary.

As I leave my bedroom, I look again at the neglected pile of shirts on my floor. My clothes, as I wear them, are useful and beautiful. On the floor they are neither. So I bend to pick them up. As I do, I notice that as I quiet their voices, I more clearly hear my own.

Discover Your Own Pearls

Find something you want to clear out this week — a closet, a drawer or even just a small corner of your room. Look at the space before you clean it and see what it has to say to you. Why is the clutter there? What does it offer and what does it take away from your life? Then de-clutter and see how you feel about that same space and how it now speaks to you. Notice if your energy changes.

DAILY DOSE

"(Good) habits are at first cobwebs, then cables."
—Spanish Proverb

I was lying on the couch on the second day of the school year, blowing my nose and feeling muscles ache that I didn't even know I had, trying to figure it out. It made no sense that I was sick. The weather was warm and glorious. I hadn't been exposed to anyone who was sick. I'd been taking my vitamins. And besides, I NEVER get colds.

As I was musing aloud in a Sudafed stupor, my husband Charley gave me that sympathetic, indulgent look, the one that says 'I'll explain this slowly so you can figure it out because obviously your brain isn't working too well.' "When was the last time you spent some time alone?" he asked.

Alone? Well, it was summer, I had been doing things with our daughters, so of course there wasn't much time alone. He continued, "And were you exercising the last few weeks?" Exercising! Who had time for that! I was busy, you know, with the girls, freelance projects, household chores, checking my emails… And then he raised his eyebrows with a "need I say more" look and walked away.

He knew I got it. Somewhere in the rush of my daily life, I had forgotten my vitamins. No, not those hard, green tablets. I had forgotten to keep up with my daily dose of those things that sustain me, that keep me in tune with myself. These are the five or six things we need to have consistently or we start to weaken, to lose touch with ourselves, to lose vitality.

So, I lugged myself off the couch, box of tissues in hand, pulled out my journal and started trying to figure out what my own daily dose would look like — what did I need and how much?

As Charley had mentioned, exercise was one. A dose of 30 minutes a day helps keep my energy up, as does limiting carbs and sugar. Next is heart-connected time with family and friends. Then there's time outside in natural light and air. And finally is time alone each day for meditation and spiritual reading, along with a good dose of "tune-ups" where I stop, breathe, listen to my body and check in with my feelings.

That's it, five things. Not too hard, yet when life comes along, I can forget exercising and instead answer emails. Or forget that time alone is essential, and instead volunteer at the school. Or forget all of them. The consequences? I can grow impatient or numb, my world shrinks and I don't experience life as deeply or vibrantly. Eventually, I may even get sick, I thought as I reached for my second glass of orange juice.

One woman I talked to said, "Often I will just blow up and lose my temper before finally taking the time for whatever it is that I am missing." And what would that be? Her daily dose is meditation, reading affirmations, 8 hours of sleep, a healthy smoothie for breakfast and physical pleasure. Another friend has a different list. She needs the ritual of making her bed immediately upon arising, time with her dog, quiet time alone, writing nightly in a gratitude journal and connections with others. My husband's list is time alone for creative projects with his hands, exercise, journaling, and hang out time with the family.

While everyone's lists sound wonderful, they're not what's essential for me. It's my daily dose that I need to keep up with. Even post on the bathroom mirror. Because life has a way of getting busy and throwing out all kinds of distractions, and before you know it you're wilting because you haven't been rooted to what's essential. We all forget our vitamins from time to time. But if they're consistently forgotten, it leads not to a day lost, but to a life not fully lived.

Discover Your Own Pearls

Take a few minutes and figure out your "daily five." Perhaps you're already doing some of them consistently; if not, now's the time to look at those things that keep you vital and connected with yourself. Add one a week — just a few minutes a day — until you reach four or five. Don't overwhelm yourself, but don't underestimate yourself, either...

LIVING IN THE PAUSE

"Now and then it's good to pause in our pursuit of happiness
and just be happy."
— Guillaume Apollinaire

Have you ever tried looking at your life upside down? Take to-do lists, for instance. We're used to looking at our daily lists for confirmation we've accomplished something. Eighteen checks is a good day. Only two? We bombed.

But what if we judged a successful day not by the tasks performed, but by the distractions? Didn't finish your laundry today because you took a nap? Woo hoo! The dusting took three hours instead of one because you stopped to play Scrabble with your kids? Way to go!

Just imagine if staying on a task, beginning to end, was a sign of failure? What if the Puritan work ethic was... wrong?

The other day I was tackling a mountain of filing that was growing like kudzu in my inbox. I had to leave for a writer's tea in an hour. Time was limited. Then my sister called. It was important, she said. I looked at the pile, every inch of me yearning to make it disappear. Then I heard my sister's voice and with a sigh abandoned it for a conversation on the front porch.

An hour later, driving to the tea, I thought about how I had released the project in favor of the conversation. At first I scolded myself. Then I remembered the words of Artur

Schnabel as he discussed piano playing. "The notes I handle no better than many pianists," he said. "But the pauses between the notes — ah, that is where the art resides!"

Exactly, I thought. It is the pauses between the notes — or in this case, meaningful meanderings in the middle of tasks — where what's worthwhile lies. Sometimes we get caught up in our "human doing" side and lose track of our equally important "human being" side.

Pauses like the one with my sister shift me from a thinking, task orientation to a feeling, people orientation. I call those "people pauses." That's where I'm paying the bills, totally focused, and my daughter Chloe will come and sit on my lap and ask where her pet goldfish went when it died. I want to finish the bills; I need to talk with her. So, I shift focus for 10 minutes. Nothing gets checked off my to-do list immediately, but everything that is important happens. When I hold too tightly onto the expectation of completing my list in a certain way and certain time frame, it doesn't open me to all the possibilities for a richer, more heart-centered life that come up along the way.

The other day an item in my planner was to brush the dog. As I slid the comb over his coat in the back yard, I noticed his gaze move towards the sky. I looked up, too, and saw two striking red birds swooping through the early morning sky before diving behind a scarlet-tipped bush. I was struck by the beauty. Had I intently stayed focused on finishing my task, I would have missed a moment of grace. A "beauty pause."

Other times, our pauses are about going inward when we've been too "outward." I can be in the middle of a project with others and find myself getting angrier and angrier about something. Then I remember the "breathing pause." I'll leave and take some deep, calming breaths. I gather myself in, like a bird drawing in disparate twigs for a nest, and feel myself coming together again. I go back out a different person. By stopping to be a human "just being," I'm able to be a better human while I'm doing.

"Gratitude pauses" also catch me sometimes. I may be in the shower sudsing when I notice the light shining through the steam and suddenly appreciate that we have money for electricity, for water and even cash to feed the dog who sleeps by the bathroom door.

So at the end of the day, what if we gave ourselves a pat on the back instead of a scolding when only two items are checked off? What if we look back at everything that wasn't on the list to begin with, and yet happened nevertheless? The hugs. The moment admiring the first spring bloom. The sweet snatches of solitude where we paused, remembering why we're here on Earth.

That's when we stop and add another line to our list. It reads "Life well lived." Check.

Discover Your Own Pearls

Next time you're in the middle of a task, notice if you're rigidly attached to finishing it in a certain way and in a certain time frame? It's fine to plan, but if you need to stop for a moment, can you? Or do you bulldoze through with casualties (including yourself) on the roadside?

QUICK STRESS FIXES

"The time to relax is when you don't have time for it."
— Sydney J. Harris

You know the gig. Dinner guests are arriving in ten minutes, a strange smell is wafting from the oven and the dog has darted inside, leaving a trail of mud in his wake. What do you do?

You can scream at your spouse that it's all his fault — even though he's in Milwaukee on a business trip. You can suck it in and explode later — perhaps in the middle of the takeout pizza that arrives to replace the burnt chicken. Or you can go for the "quick stress fix." The one I pull out many times each day, whenever needed, whatever the circumstances.

I have a whole arsenal of them. The common denominator is that they must be quick and possible to use anywhere, anytime. Often they're not a cure, but at least the bleeding stops — deeper solutions can come later.

The simplest one is breathing. You know, that thing we almost stop doing when under stress. Suddenly we find ourselves ventilating more like hummingbirds than humans. So, I take a few deep, diaphragmatic breaths right in the middle of any situation. If I can escape and do it someplace quiet, even better. My friend Eileen takes it one step further and breathes into areas of her body that are tense. "The oxygenation actually helps to loosen things up and break down the stress," she says.

Stay-at-home mom Adrienne adds another twist. "My regular coping tool is taking a deep, deep breath, and then blowing out my frustrations. Immediately following, I take another deep breath, thanking Creator for all my blessings and for my trust that all is in Divine order. I do that as often as necessary, some days more than others," she says.

Other quick stress fixes revolve around a mantra or philosophy of life. A former nurse still uses a few lines she learned while working. When she starts to lose it, she asks herself, "Is anybody dead? No. Will it matter in 10 years? No. Then let it go."

My mother wore a handmade Greek prayer bracelet and would relax by repeating the traditional Jesus prayer, which goes, "Lord Jesus Christ, have mercy upon me." One mom says she releases her "small" cares and feels peace in the middle of her day when she silently repeats the Prayer of Protection to herself: "The light of God surrounds me. The love of God enfolds me. The power of God protects me and the presence of God watches over me. Wherever I am, God is. And all is well."

Some fixes are more physical. My daughter Alix releases anxiety with a quick 50-yard dash. A yoga teacher I know shakes out stress with a forward bend. Sandi, an animal lover, has a cure that she can do even when her living room is full of company. She pets her big, friendly dog. "Petting him is sheer bliss and does more to center me than any kind of meditation, yoga or self-talk," she claims. "He has a wonderful essence that makes me feel loved, safe and strong."

Other times, I'm not in an immediately stressful situation, but I just feel out of whack. Perhaps a bit anxious or uncomfortable for no obvious reason. That's when I do the one-minute splat. In a pinch I do it mentally — otherwise, on paper. I splat all my problems and fears on a page, from the serious (illness) to the trivial (I can't find my nail clipper and I've looked everywhere!). Just the act of shining a light on my "problems," rather than letting them taunt me from the shadows, shrinks them to a size I can manage.

One of my favorite quick stress cures is mentally stepping

out of a situation and observing. There's a big difference between being caught up in an emotion or event, and stepping back and watching it with compassion, knowing it will pass. Say I'm angry at the dog. Instead of just being mad, I first notice that I'm angry, then fully accept and embrace that emotion. That acceptance alone starts defusing it. Then I quickly scan my body for tense areas and also observe the often incorrect "stories" I'm telling myself about the situation. This takes only about a minute, but the results are huge.

The trick is to find a method or two that works for you, and then use it so consistently that it almost becomes second nature, appearing when you most need it. From one small practice can grow a more peaceful response towards life, one with more joy, less pain. You may not be able to save the chicken from burning at your dinner party, but at least the smoke will be coming from your oven, not your ears.

Discover Your Own Pearls

Choose any one of the quick stress fixes mentioned here, or one of your own, and try it for a couple of days when you feel yourself getting off balance. Then choose another and try it for a couple of days. Keep going until you find one that "clicks" for you.

OH, THE STORIES WE TELL

"All misery begins in the mind, fueled by the stories we tell ourselves about what should have happened, what ought to happen, etc. Listen to your mind. What story is it telling you? Does the story make you feel better or worse? Just notice the story. Calling your pain "the pain" instead of "my pain" will shift your perception toward easier release. Keep breathing."
— Christiane Northrup, M.D.

By the time they reached the San Antonio motel at midnight, the high school debate team was exhausted. My daughter Alix and three other girls crammed into the tiny room and tried to sleep but couldn't. The next day, Alix's voice became raspy from a worsening cold and nervous knots punched her stomach as she debated. By the time she returned to Austin at 2 a.m., slowed by torrential rains that hit the Texas coast, she was a crumpled heap — sick, tired, cranky. It was an unpleasant scene… and one that never happened.

The debate that weekend was cancelled due to Hurricane Rita, but I had a full week beforehand to live through it, over and over, in my imagination. All I needed were a few crumbs — the hint of illness, potential bad weather, late hours — and I was able to create a whole story in my head that I was sure was nothing less than truth.

"I often use the word 'story' to talk about thoughts, or sequences of thoughts, that we convince ourselves are real," says author Byron Katie. "A story may be about the past, the present, or the future; it may be about what things should be, what they could be, or why they are. Stories appear in our minds hundreds of times a day." Problem is, these stories are often not true, yet they create anxiety as if they were.

Growing up half Greek, telling stories came naturally. The more drama the better. Give me any molehill and I'll find a mountain. But I'm discovering that the drama and interest they generate aren't worth the price of the stress.

Now, stories aren't just within the dramatic among us. You've got 'em, too. See if any of these resonate. Aunt Bee never returned your phone call — she must be mad because you forgot her birthday last year. Your son is late getting home from his party — he must not really care about you. Your throat is scratchy — not only are you catching a cold, but it'll ruin your presentation on Tuesday and likely drag on for weeks, just like last time.

First you have the fact — your throat is scratchy — and then the fiction. And oh, what fiction we create. Not only big, bodacious tales, but also little stories that grow in our minds before we even notice them.

When I woke up this morning, I was feeling more tired than usual. I heard animated chatting coming from the kitchen. In a nanosecond, I had a story. I saw how I would go in the kitchen and have to deal with those "cheerful" people, and what a disaster it would be. I was already predicting the future, minus an accurate crystal ball.

This time, though, instead of getting caught like a fly in a sticky story web, I extricated myself. Just by watching myself spin this tale, I was able to drop it and walk in the kitchen without my defenses up, without judgment, ready for whatever may happen at that moment. Good or bad.

So why bother to catch yourself telling a story? Besides the obvious downside of the stress it creates, there's another negative. It takes you out of the moment. American Buddhist nun Pema Chodron says, "We can train in letting the story line go. Slow down enough just to be present, let go of the multitude of judgments and schemes, and stop struggling."

Ah, relax into life as it is, not as we imagine it to be.

When I had concocted Alix's potentially disastrous debate outing, I was in my head and out of the moment. When I recognized it as a story, I came back home. I found myself curled up in the warm colors of my oversized chair with a steaming cup of chai tea. I felt the rough fabric of the chair, the cool air sliding in from a cracked window. In other words, I got that little piece of my life back.

So, how do we release these stories? How do we go from cluttered mind to peaceful appreciation of the soft slippers we're wearing? Ideally, we'd be aware of our thoughts all the time. However, most of us wait until we feel an uncomfortable emotion before we start paying attention. That's my signal to look within and see what faulty thoughts are running through my brain. Just observing with a bit of lightness reduces the story's power. "Ah, Carolyn, there's that debate fiasco story again. How interesting."

As for Alix's debate, it's now been rescheduled. I fret about the three hour ride on an old school bus without toilets... certain disaster. Then I stop and chuckle at myself. I gently blow away the story web and find myself outside, inhaling the smell of nearby rain as I brush our dog's apricot coat. For this moment, the debate has been won.

Discover Your Own Pearls

Whenever you feel yourself start to get upset, anxious or off center, pause for a moment and see what story is running through your head. You can't release thoughts you don't see in the first place, so start by just observing them. Gently look and see what's there. What beliefs are floating around? Are they ones you want to keep, or release?...

EARLY BIRD OR NIGHT OWL?

"Their (night people) membership boasts the likes of Andy Warhol,
Missy Elliott and Lenny Kravitz, while morning people are lumped
in with Katie Couric and Ned Flanders."
— Patrick Quirk

It should have been obvious the first time my husband Charley and I met. A friend from a writer's group had convinced me to check out an early morning Toastmaster's group, and with a wink said there were a lot of cute guys there. So I grudgingly pulled myself out of bed at 5:45 a.m., stumbled into the meeting barely dressed, and sidestepped his cheery hello to lunge at the coffee. As the meeting progressed, Charley percolated intelligent words and presented impromptu speeches with witty analogies and insight. I barely grunted good morning.

Almost 20 years later, things haven't changed much.

He's a morning person, I'm a night one. They say opposites attract, and perhaps what that really means is not passive verses fiery or quiche verses steak, but morning verses night.

Anywhere between 4:30 and 6 a.m., he's rolling out of bed to do whatever one does at that hour. I wouldn't know. I'm asleep. Come evening, my husband doesn't just sleep when he's tired. He has to preface his exit with something like "5 a.m. sure came early today" so I won't accuse him of being lazy or a party pooper for going to bed when the grandpas of the world are shutting out their lights. What he doesn't realize is that I won't judge him for going to bed early... if he won't judge me for sleeping in on weekends.

Some couples with this incompatibility argue about it. They feel one tendency is inherently better than the other. Usually the morning person feels virtuous about having gotten "half the day over with" before the lingering spouse rolls out of bed. They'll tick off their accomplishments with glee, from walking the dog to downing their protein shake hours ago or finishing the newspaper crossword puzzle. Revenge for such behavior doesn't come until night, when the main band is just coming on and they've missed it, having dozed off into their drink. Or when the spouse snoozes through Letterman's Top 10. Of course, they can watch all the exciting offerings on TV when they wake up — like predawn fishing shows.

While some are annoyed by these differences, other couples downright cherish them because it means one thing — time alone. My friend Meeta says she often wakes up to an empty bed and finds her husband awake and happily "reading or reconfiguring the miles of wire that feed into the media room." As mother of two daughters, she adds, "Quiet time is what he treasures most, especially in a house of constantly chattering females. As long as he's up to drop them off in the morning, I don't grudge him his little slice of nirvana."

Couples on the same sleep cycle get a different benefit — intimate time together. One "morning couple" carves time for themselves over coffee while their sons sleep. That wouldn't work for us. As luck would have it, our kids are on different cycles, too. On weekends, who's popping out of what door — and when — is as complicated as a three-ring circus. One daughter rises early and is literally singing and bright-eyed within 30 seconds. The other one would happily wake up to "good afternoon" instead of "good morning." Even the dog has his own cycle.

Try as we might, there's not much point fighting it. According to Dr. Simon Archer, who led a University of Surry study about sleep, cycles may be genetically programmed. "We found most of the extreme morning preference people have the longer (Period 3) gene and the extreme evening preference people have the short gene," says Archer. So although I may try to rise with the sun and meditate, my body is more wired to bask under the stars and contemplate. My companions are hoot owls, not robins.

Either way, what we're all looking for is "bonus time" on either end of the clock. Time when the world is slower, quieter. When we're not fighting traffic or punching a clock. Early morning offers a sense of possibility; late evening, closure and gratitude. We all want to steal just a bit more pleasure from life. Happily, that gift offers itself 24 hours a day.

Discover Your Own Pearls

Are you a night or a morning person? What about your spouse or kids? How does this affect time together — does it give you more intimate time with others in your family or more time alone? Are you happy with this mix or do you inwardly feel resentful about it? How can you use your morning or evening orientation as an asset in your life?

ALL SYSTEMS GO

*"In order to seek one's own direction, one must simplify the
mechanics of ordinary, everyday life."*
— Plato

The roll of the eyes said it all. Here she goes again, my daughters thought as they watched me wave towards the "needs to go upstairs" pile on the stairway. You see all this stuff, I asked. I'd like it to disappear. All you have to do, I brightly continued despite the lethal stares, is pick something up every time you go upstairs, and as you're walking upstairs shake this maraca. Everyone in hearing distance will cheer for you, and the steps will be clean!

You see, I added with the passion of the newly-converted, everything comes down to a system. This will be called the "Stop and Maraca" system. Now, let's move on to the laundry room...

Laugh if you will, but these and other harebrained ideas have become the key to my sanity. Until recently, I had no idea what it was that separated me, the "domestically challenged," from those women who glided through their days leaving polished coffee tables and clutter-free closets in their wake. They must have full-time housekeepers, I mused. Or they're natural neatniks, a genetic disposition I'd never been blessed with. Perhaps something in their birth order foretold of domestic order? I puzzled and pondered until one day I came up with the deceptively simple answer. They had systems; I didn't.

While I was trying to round up distracted daughters before school, shouting "watch the time" as I spread peanut butter on bread and stumbled over wayward SuperBalls, other women were sipping tea. The difference? They had the "Before School Ready Routine" down pat. They had a system for lunches (packed the night before during dinner clean-up) and a system for backpacks (always kept with other school accessories on a specially designated table). Their mornings happened with the precision of a Swiss timepiece; mine was more akin to a cuckoo clock.

Once I realized that putting a few systems in place would help turn my home into the orderly dream retreat I'd always envisioned, I was hooked. Systems started popping up like wildflowers in our house, sprouting from the laundry room to the bathroom. Some blossomed; others wilted. During the "Hula Hoop Cleaning" method, my daughter tossed the hoop in her room and cleaned out everything it encircled, but a few dresser-top knickknacks became causalities from the flying cleaning device. It was replaced with the "Basket Cleaning" system, where the room is instantly transformed by putting everything left out into a laundry basket. Then, every day she puts away 10 items from the basket. So far, so good.

Most of our systems are homemade, but we've also started poking around magazines for ideas. Some worked (the errand drawer), others were downright laughable, such as freeing counter space by hanging 20 cereal boxes on the wall for various files.

There are always the failed systems — the charts with stars, the shoe organizer — but those memories recede as we fall in love with our newest system, a bright, shiny spot of simplicity lighting our days. The thrill of finding systems that work is greater than any packaged gift. Each one bestows its own reward by saving time, energy, stress or all three. Systems even save wear on relationships. You want to watch TV before homework? You know the "Homework First" system, don't you? Then, your child's anger is directed at the "the System," a mustachioed villain in the drama, while you smile innocently and continue knitting.

I'm still getting the hang of this systems thing, though. Still working out the kinks — and there always will be kinks — and learning more from the masters. One is my friend Sandi. She not only has those everyday, run-of-the-mill systems down, like the "Grocery List on the Fridge" one and the "Gardening Tools" one, but she's also moved on to a higher level, putting systems in place that help create the life she wants. She loves people stopping in and visiting, so she's created a system to welcome guests, have their rooms ready and file their preferences for next visit. All of this leads to more visitors, which is exactly what she wants!

Just thinking of the possibilities makes me giddy. Imagine the "Dinner Party in Two Minutes" one, or the "Mom's After Dinner Aromatherapy Bath" system. But for now, I think I'm happy with the "Mom's not Quite as Stressed Because of her Systems" system.

Discover Your Own Pearls

What drives you nuts? The dishes always left out in the dish rack? The unsorted socks in a basket by the bed? The pandemonium before dinner? Pick one thing, then find a system (make one up or research books/internet) to help solve that problem. Be creative and have fun doing it. If your energy increases once the system is in place, it's a keeper!

LESSONS FROM THE LABRADOR

"The judging mind has an opinion about everything. It selects from the mindflow who it believes it ought to be and chides the rest. It's full of noise and old learning. It is a quality of mind addicted to maintaining an image of itself. It is always trying to be somebody."
— Stephen Levine

Yesterday I was spinning plates. You know the feeling. Everything was going right. I was caught up on all my writing assignments, I had lost a few pounds, my hair actually did what it was supposed to and I was excited about some new projects. I had every one of those plates up and spinning and was feeling pretty smug.

My self-talk was sounding like this — you know, Carolyn, you're a pretty cool person. You have it together. The sky's the limit and you can do anything. You go, girl!

It seemed like they'd spin forever.

It always does…

Two hours later, they came crashing down. I had signed up for an important tele-class, even changing a doctor's appointment so I could participate. But right before the class started, I realized in panic that I'd never received the phone number. With a sinking feeling, I tried calling the organization sponsoring the call. An answering machine clicked on. I e-mailed. No reply.

An hour later, with only 20 minutes left in the class, the registrar finally called with the phone number and an apology.

I quickly dialed in, trying to ignore my dog who realized I was otherwise occupied and began gleefully shredding an empty carton he'd found. Right about the time he finished scattering the paper, my cordless phone lost its charge and I was disconnected. There were 10 minutes left in the class.

The whole experience had been stressful, but now it got worse. I started thinking about it. You'll never amount to anything, you can't even succeed at making one call, the voices in my head screamed. You're a technological idiot. Where are your priorities, you should have stuck with your doctor's appointment. Plus, you look fat today!

Just as the voices were going full throttle, not only beating me up but dipping deeper into a well of all the unworthy feelings I'd ever had, I noticed the dog. He was contentedly lying amid his paper carnage. He wasn't telling himself how he was addicted to shredding things and would never break that habit. He sure didn't look like he was guiltily recollecting the time he'd peed in our upstairs den, or taken his toys outside only to forget them in the rain.

Yet that's exactly what we do… constantly. It takes only the slightest slip, the merest whisper, for us to find some way to judge ourselves. The scary thing is that most of the time we don't even notice it. We find ourselves feeling lousy, but unless we have the presence of mind to then stop, examining the thoughts going through our head like background Muzak, we don't know why we feel bad. You forgot to send your child out with their lunch, the negative voice in our head says. What kind of mother are you! You had a fender bender with another vehicle? You're getting old and should be taken off the road!

Once we catch the voice, we can see the silly over-inflation for what it is. A missed class doesn't make me an idiot. It surely doesn't make me fat. In fact, I'm exactly the same person I was two hours earlier, when I was reveling in my wonderful-ness.

As our dog padded across the wood floor to settle into a session of bone chewing, I thought how matter-of-factly and good-naturedly he approached everything. There's no drama with him. No judgment. In fact, as little "thinking" as possible.

He doesn't kick himself when he's down; nor does he over-inflate himself to feel good. Wow, I'm catching more flies than any dog on the block! This shaggy coat of mine would sure look good in the movies!

No, he just accepts himself — as is — and gets on with his life.

He's a good teacher. I don't need to spin plates to consider myself worthy. A dropped plate is not a sign of unworthiness. It's just a dropped plate. Period. Or, like the dog, it's just another opportunity to lick up what spills and move on.

Discover Your Own Pearls

Next time you find yourself irritated, sad or uncomfortable in some way, stop a moment and tune in. What are you telling yourself? Literally, what are the words going through your head? Are they true? Are you sure? More than likely, they're some outworn fear, belief or habit that, if you write out or look at closely, you'll discover isn't true for you.

FOR THE LOVE OF BOOKS

"She is too fond of books, and it has addled her brain."
— Louisa May Alcott

I've been having affairs for years. My husband, kindly, looks the other way. He tolerates it when I steal away for an afternoon. Or when I share my bed. Because he knows that after these interludes I always come back to him. After all, he's a man. My companions are man-made... they're books.

Walking into my house, signs of the affair are obvious — a book lies open on a pillow while another, split with a crimson bookmark, lounges on the couch. One need only peer onto my bookshelves to see the intimacies I've had through the years. A carefree "Zorba the Greek" cozies up to no-nonsense "Is there Life after Housework?," just a shelf away from a splattered copy of "Creative Mosaics" and "The Crazy Dog Guide to Happier Work." Spiritual texts find no offense residing next to murder mysteries, while Dylan Thomas' overwrought love poems bump up to responsible parenting books.

Each changed my life, enriched it, enlarged it in a way that nothing else can. Books are integral to who I am. Sometimes they massage my brain cells, other times I come across wisdom so profound that the course of my existence is forever altered. And then again, sometimes they're just good for a laugh.

I even love the feel of books, fresh from the bookstore, the pages smooth, cool and virginal. Anticipation mounts as the read begins. But after spending time together, sometimes you find the company dull. The cover may have been appealing, all mod clothes and bright colors, but the inside just doesn't deliver. Other times, though, the inside lights you with inspiration. You laugh and cry and can't understand how the words on the page so perfectly mirror the thoughts you feared were yours alone.

I've had everything from one-night-stands to long-term relationships. The former are usually novels in crinkly cellophane covers, dragged home from the library for a day or a week and then returned, sometimes even forgotten, no matter how torrid our time together. Others have stayed in my home for years. They are no longer pristine, but I love every scar, can trace my hand over the creased, dog-eared pages and along the rough, cracked, binding. Underlined passages call for another read. Another pleasure.

Perusing my bookshelves, I spot a small green and orange book with Snoopy lying contentedly on his doghouse. It was a gift from my mother to me at age 11, and inside, the inscription in part reads "Thanks for being you... I love you googol times." Next to it is one with a personal note from the late actor Anthony Quinn, written as we ate migas and chatted for an interview at a seaside café. Scattered throughout my shelves, these inscribed books carry poignant memories of people and times together, their warmth lingering amidst the pages.

Books can connect you with the giver, but they also connect you with the writer. I love the idea that someone can write a book in the woods at the northern edge of Minnesota, a snowstorm whirling around them, and I can read that same book on the edge of Barton Springs, pages flecked with water from splashing swimmers. In fact, where you are when you read subtly changes your experience. It's one thing to read in bed around midnight with a book light; quite another to sit outside on a porch, squinting with the glare of the sunlight, winter toes warming in the sun as your eyes move along the passages.

Fiction takes me on ocean swells to other places; nonfiction satisfies an ever curious mind. When life challenges come up, there's always a book to satiate my desire. Recently, I was sleeping only sporadically, so books on insomnia began multiplying on my bedside table. A quickie isn't enough for me — I like the vast spread of knowledge. I wrapped myself around those pages for days, learning about circadian rhythms, how deep delta sleep decreases as you age and about a woman who stayed in cave for more than four months, eventually waking daily for 23 hours and sleeping for 10 — and all the while she stormed through 400 books! I come across information both helpful and whimsical on these fact-finding sprees as my life grows richer, broader, more interesting.

My daughters are now book lovers, too. I still remember Alix's last day of fourth grade, when the school librarian gave her a special invitation. She let her spend two hours alone in the library, picking out her summer reads. In the end, she hauled out boxes filled with booty. It was dizzying, the selection — books fat and thin, mysterious and practical, exciting and preachy — all waiting to spend time with her on a languid summer's day. I wanted more than anything to roam among the books myself, to pick them out for her. Yet, as any parent knows, you have to let your children go. Let them choose. I'm just glad my girls chose a love where the adventures are deep, expansive and satisfying — and one which won't leave them in the morning.

Discover Your Own Pearls

Are you happy with the amount of time you give yourself to read? Is it always five minutes before bed, when you're too tired to truly enjoy the book? If you wish you had more time, make it a priority. Carve out some time this week, just for you, to enjoy reading — in front of a fire with a cup of tea, or outside on a lawn chair. Indulge...

SORTING IT OUT

"The average 3-bedroom home has 350,000 things in it."
— Lanna Nakone, M.A.

The sock drawer says it all. Some people not only roll their socks, but separate dressy from casual, light from dark. These are the same people who have their address books flawlessly updated and a scheduled day of the week for dusting the lampshades.

Not our family. Here, everyone's socks go directly from the dryer into a communal, unsorted drawer. Mornings before school we gather 'round the "sock spot," chatting about the upcoming day while foraging for a matching pair. Sometimes the dog will poke his nose in and steal one, but by and large this system works. For us. And now I understand why.

At first, I was envious of those sock rollers. Why didn't that inclination come naturally to me, I wondered? Perhaps if I figured that out, the light would also dawn on how to easily file recipes and follow a budget. In my quest for organizational enlightenment, I decided to hire a professional organizer.

I had met one at a conference a few months ago. What was her name? Vanessa something? I just couldn't remember, but I knew I had her card. Somewhere. Usually I tossed business cards in a kitchen drawer, but sometimes they landed in the front hall drawer. Unless they had slipped behind a chair...

The next week the organizer arrived. As she studiously

walked through the house, pen in hand and brows furrowed, she finally managed to cheerfully sputter, "Well, you certainly have a very... ah... busy, energetic and creative household!"

I knew what that meant.

As it turns out, I have a good excuse for my less than finicky proclivities. I happened upon the answer one day at the bookstore when I spotted a copy of "Organizing For Your Brain Type." According the author, the brain's cerebral cortex is broken down into four essentially equal sized areas, and each has a different way of processing information. Evidently, some of us are naturally inclined towards organization and routine.

Then there are the rest of us.

I'm what's called a "harmonizer," a right-brain type the author tactfully says "has an in-the-moment attitude to time management." That explains why my left-brain friends can happily exercise at the same time each day, week in and week out, while I'm about as unpredictable as the local weather.

Harmonizers also prefer people over things. Traditional organizers can quickly purge what isn't needed. But when I clean, books and knick knacks go in the back of the car to deliver to friends who would enjoy them. And while left-brain types can buy gifts months in advance and store them in a consistent spot, I often can't. It's hard enough to stifle my excitement and resist giving a birthday gift before the date. Even if I manage to "hide" it, half the time I never find it again. I'm sure one day someone will find a treasure trove of lip glosses inside a sweater in the guest closet.

But there's another side to the story as well. Right-brain types may misplace the wine-opener for the party, but we can create an atmosphere that's lively and fun. What we lack in consistency we make up for in creativity. And we can get rid of clutter as well as anyone else — we just may do it relay race-style with everyone in the family rather than the way suggested by traditional organizing books.

Getting organized — my way — has become a fascinating adventure. My "mail system" has become a simple wicker basket near the door. Once nomadic business cards are quietly settling into a large folder. And exercise happens, even though it's sometimes on the fly, rather than on the dot.

As for our family's socks, they'll likely continue to be a colorful cotton jungle in a giant drawer. It's possible I'll sort them one day — right after I alphabetize my coupons.

Discover Your Own Pearls

What is your organizing style? Are you more the "maintaining style" (develops and follows routines well and does best with traditional organizing methods) or the "innovating style" (artistic and creative with a "stacking system" no one else understands). There are other styles, too, but these are the two extremes. Are you honoring your particular style, or trying to force yourself into a style that doesn't fit? What one organizing step can you take that would help you feel more peaceful? Sorting through a certain closet? A drawer? Do it!

WALK, DON'T WOBBLE

"Multitasking means screwing up several things at once."
— Unknown

She must have been steering with her knee, because the brunette in the Volvo next to me was holding a sandwich in one hand while talking on her cell phone with the other. A rock song slid out through the crack of open window. I was going to slow down to steer clear of her, but I didn't have to — the next moment she shot ahead of me.

As I watched the smoke from her tailpipe disappear, words came to me that I had read long ago by Buddha. "If you walk, walk. If you sit, sit. Don't wobble."

Over the next few weeks, that message about doing one thing at a time — with complete focus — kept popping in my head. Suddenly, I started seeing how I snuck in snatches of a novel while my daughter Chloe cartwheeled through gymnastics. My turkey sandwich somehow disappeared while watching the news. I stir-fried dinner while drilling math facts. I was, in a word, wobbling.

The worst were those mornings when everyone was getting ready for school — a sock here, a bite of eggs there, my husband dashing out the door with a cup of coffee. Some days I even had the lunacy to try and read the paper and check e-mails in staccato bursts between requests. Yet, when everyone had left, I somehow felt empty. I wouldn't see my family all day, yet I had been juggling so many balls that I hadn't stopped long enough to notice a daughter ready early and loitering around the staircase, just aching for a hug. Or to focus for a few seconds to give my husband a kiss goodbye that meant something, rather than blowing one from behind the banister as he disappeared. We wobbled so much those mornings it's amazing we didn't land flat on our faces.

Even when I was doing just one task, I found wobbles. Mental wobbles. You know, when your body is doing a reasonable imitation of "interested listener," while your mind is worrying about where you put your keys, or why you ate those chilies for breakfast.

Rather than living as deeply as I could, all this multi-tasking was rounding out the edges of my day, sandpapering it down, homogenizing it. Rather than experiencing more highs from wholehearted, conscious attention — which makes even the mundane seem magical — I put up with days of low level stress and anxiety that percolated up when I did too many mindless, half-hearted activities.

Yet, when I put my attention on "sitting" instead of "wobbling," I was gifted with tiny treasures throughout the day. When I took walks without my headset on, I started smelling the gardenias in the air and chatting with neighbors. Eating alone was sensually sweet and lip pucker sour. Cartwheels spun and thunked in my brain as I zoomed in on Chloe's gymnastics. Life seemed so much more direct. Precious. Profound.

I remember the long hours nursing my daughter when she was a baby. Usually, I'd feed her and read. What I read, I can't recall. But I do remember the times when I put the book down and really paid attention. I remember the tiny freckle on her temple throbbing as she sucked, the pale sheen of her skin, the feathery wisps of brown hair. I remember her drunken milk grin as she lay heavy and satiated in my arms, a dribble of white trickling down her chin. This wasn't the blur of multitasking, but the permanent brand of a moment fully lived.

Wobbling is part of life, but at least now I do it less out of habit and more as a conscious decision whose price I understand. And sometimes I'll be going full tilt, mindlessly speeding through life, when a giant stop sign will appear in my head. I'll put down the drink and cell phone and focus instead on the drive. When you're fully there, it's one heck of a view.

Discover Your Own Pearls

Observe when you're trying to do several things at a time and see how it makes you feel. How does your body feel? Are you content or stressed? Tuned in or out? Then, try to fully focus on one activity and see what happens. Put all your attention on it, then switch to the next activity. How did your experience change?

Holiday Pearls

CATCHING CHRISTMAS SPIRIT

*"Until one feels the spirit of Christmas, there is no Christmas.
All else is outward display -- so much tinsel and decorations. For it
isn't the holly, it isn't the snow. It isn't the tree not the firelight's
glow. It's the warmth that comes to the hearts of men when the
Christmas spirit returns again."*
—Unknown

It seems I would have learned by now. Every year I set tinsel traps to entice my seasonal prey — Christmas Spirit. I spread out eggnog and red-sprinkled cookies, hang mistletoe and play "Jingle Bells" while shining party dishes. But no matter. The more I try to lasso it with a yard of ribbon and a ho ho ho, the more it eludes me.

This year, the bait of choice was nearby Fredericksburg. It would be the perfect spot for catching the spirit of the season, I explained to my family as we climbed into the mini-van for the trek west. I could already see us all laughing and strolling down quaint holiday streets, dipping in for a hot chocolate here, a peppermint there, the children's eyes aglow beside holiday windows.

Of course, the reality check didn't take long. We waited, along with half of Texas, in a line of cars slowly snaking into the city's holiday wrapped core. Then we toured Main Street — over, and over, and over again as we searched for an elusive parking spot. By the time we started walking, my youngest daughter decided she'd had enough fun for the day and was ready to head home.

A few exhausting hours later, we surrendered and began the drive home — but not before a stop at nearby Enchanted Rock. I clearly remember my less-than-storybook-happy mood as we started hiking and my husband Charley asked me if I had the camera. Of course not, I replied a tad edgily. After all, photos are for times you actually want to remember...

So, we plodded up the mountain, bad moods and all. But somehow, the further up we went, the more bounce there was to our step. We forgot about trying to make it the perfect holiday experience and instead focused on climbing, breathing, opening.

As we neared the top, the last of an orange sunset was fringing the horizon and the tip of the adjacent peak was glowing reddish orange. We could hear late season crickets in the bushes. A crescent moon lazily reclined in the darkening sky.

That's when I realized that the peace and joy we had vainly searched for in shop windows had quietly arrived when we least expected it. Christmas spirit had been waiting for us all along at the top of this pink granite dome — or had it been with us the whole time, but we were so busy trying to script its appearance that we couldn't see it?

Eventually, we left the embrace of that vast, silent night and drove through the darkness looking for a meal. We headed for a pizza parlor in Llano, but the only available parking space led us instead to the old Acme Dry Goods building, which had been converted into a rustic restaurant.

A jingling bell on the wooden door greeted travelers, and we sat beside a window overlooking a town square etched with tiny white lights and bows. As Christmas carols floated in the background, who should appear before our eyes but... Santa? He said he was the chef, but with that white beard, round belly and his assertion that he could create anything the girls could imagine, we wondered. Besides, those waiters did seem to have awfully pointy ears. And he chuckled as he brought us dessert — a bowl full of Jelly Bellies.

Christmas spirit held us close that evening, from the starry skies above Enchanted Rock to an imaginative detour in a cozy café. Perhaps next year I won't lure Christmas spirit at all — I'll simply put out the welcome mat, leave on the light, and wait for the magic to sneak up from behind...

Discover Your Own Pearls

Think back to past holidays and see what happy memories you can find. Do you remember what you were doing or who was with you? The brisk smell of the air, the taste of the cranberries? Take a moment and really feel it. When the holidays come around again, remember that feeling and bring it back—regardless of what's happening around you. That elusive spirit always starts on the inside.

'TIS BETTER TO RECEIVE THAN TO GIVE

"The art of acceptance is the art of making someone
who has just done you a small favor wish that
he might have done you a greater one."
— Russell Lynes

Some people may want to pin up my picture next to Scrooge's, but I'm gonna say it anyway — 'Tis better to receive than to give. Yes, you heard right. Everywhere you look the message is just the opposite, with churches, malls and charities all extolling the virtues of giving during the holidays. It's a great message — except for mothers. They have the unselfish giving gig down pat. It's the receiving that could use a little work...

For us, giving to our kids is like breathing. Imagine, for instance, that your son's school play just happens to fall on the day of the hair appointment you've waited a month to get. Your child only has one line in it. Do you go to the play, or color and cut? And after the play, when he's crying about tripping on the steps to the stage, we know just what flavor of Blue Bell ice cream will make him feel better. We know when a quiet hug and no words are necessary at the end of the school day. We know just how to rub their backs at night — even when we're falling asleep ourselves — so they can unclench cares of the day.

I was with a group of women at a workshop once and the

presenter asked what made us happy. We sat. We squirmed. We looked blankly at each other, then embarrassedly looked down at our hands. These hands that had been so busy helping every else had no idea how to help themselves, or to reach out for help. We didn't know how to ask others for what we needed, because often we didn't know ourselves. We had been too busy... giving.

My mother was strong and independent and gave voraciously. Comment that you admired a holiday decoration in her house, and by the time you got to the door it had been secretly placed in your purse. Arrive on the 2 a.m. red-eye, and she'd not only greet you at the airport, but take you home for a bowl of Greek avgolemono soup. Show her your broken heart, and she'd break her own to help mend yours. Yes, my mother would give us anything — except the joy of giving to her.

I remember when feminism started picking up steam in the 60's. My mother was excited about the movement and lectured me, over and over, to not depend on anyone. Be self-sufficient, she said. Be strong. In high school, I sported one of those t-shirts that said, "A woman without a man is like a fish without a bicycle." Like so many women, these messages led us towards independence, but with a price. We didn't want to ask for help from anyone, and didn't know how to receive it.

The heart of receiving is vulnerability. A willingness to be open and ask for help. It takes courage to believe that we're worthy enough to accept wonderful things for ourselves. It also takes a lot of self-love and acceptance — more than we have, some days.

When my mother got cancer, the pattern continued. Rather than having bottled water delivered, or letting us drop it off for her, in her weakened state she'd still schlep over to the grocery store to get it herself. But as time wore on and her cancer progressed, things slowly changed. Suddenly my invincible mother was crying, for no other reason than that she saw something beautiful and it moved her. The barriers between her and her ability to receive were dissolving. By the last week of her life, they were completely gone. As she lay in bed, we tenderly swabbed her mouth to keep it moist, put compresses on her head, rubbed her feet. We hugged her and told her how much she meant to us. When she had almost run out of a lifetime of words, she mustered a few more — a request for Haagen-Dazs chocolate ice cream. We giddily, tearfully complied.

Ultimately, this was her final and greatest gift — the ability to receive our love at its fullest.

So this year, celebrate the season to receive. Open up enough to receive all the love that others have been waiting to give you, and that you have been afraid to give to yourself. After all, if Scrooge can figure out how to give, we can certainly figure out how to receive…

Discover Your Own Pearls

Are you better at giving or receiving? Are you perhaps better at receiving in some areas of your life, but not in others? How have you affected others during the times it's been challenging to receive? You are worth it — give yourself permission to abundantly receive in all areas of your life…

THE THANKSGIVING SECRET

"Naps are the adult version of a child's fort.
A love of privacy and place for make-believe."
— Sark

There's a big Thanksgiving tradition that's kept hush-hush. It's rarely mentioned in papers, let alone around the locker room. And yet, late afternoon on Thanksgiving, you can almost hear the collective creaks of lazy boy chairs being reclined, the gentle snores just beyond the din of football games, the homemade afghans being pulled up around the chin.

It's the Thanksgiving nap, just as much an American custom as the turkey. Yet when it comes to admitting it — on Thanksgiving much less any other time of year — the forlorn nap isn't embraced like a long lost cousin. Instead, it's greeted with anything from an embarrassed chuckle to contempt. As we try to impress others with just how busy we are, naps are a little secret kept behind closed doors and underneath down comforters.

I'm not sure when napping went from being a childhood privilege to an adult shortcoming, or when we became too grown-up for the simple joy of a few quiet moments with our own breath.

We certainly had no qualms about it in kindergarten. I remember snacking with my classmates on sugar cookies and lukewarm apple juice, then lying on wrinkled blankets, squirming bodies slowly settling down, scratching last minute itches before quieting. We drifted off to the gentle hum of the air-conditioner, the birds in the trees outside, the acorns dropping.

The air-conditioner still whirred as I napped with my own babies, their warm, pudgy bodies next to mine, inhaling their sweet smell of milk-breath and baby shampoo. We had rainy day naps in darkened rooms, winter naps by the fire, spring naps with windows flung open.

When my daughters got older — shedding napping like last year's skin — I found I wasn't so ready to throw off that pleasure. Besides, they still needed mental respites in their day. So, nap time became "quiet time." TV's and computers were silenced and everyone retreated to the sanctuary of their rooms. For them, that meant an imaginative hour filled only with the clipping of rounded scissors on construction paper or the cooing of Barbie princesses teetering on Lego castles. For me, it meant climbing under down-filled covers with a cup of hot mint tea and a novel, eventually closing my eyes for 10 or 15 blissful minutes. By the time we rejoined each other, we were fully charged for the rest of the day.

Artist Paul Gauguin once said, "I shut my eyes in order to see." I like that. When we nap, we close our eyes to the jarring stimulation of the day, unclenching tightly wound minds and bodies in a way that leaves space for creative thought to enter. Right brain replaces left brain. You drift on a cloud of semi-consciousness, where images of stacked paperwork dissolve into floating pearls and pink pancakes. You lie down with a chalk board brain full of scribbles and cares, and wake up to a clean slate.

When we don't allow ourselves to nap, we say it's because we're too busy. There's no time, we rationalize. But really, it's a subtle way of depriving ourselves. We not only don't nap when we need to, we also don't lie in the grass and stare at clouds, or sit and doodle on a summer day. We've grown accustomed to marching to the siren call of purposeful activity, ignoring the gentler callings of our spirit. We've grown up.

So this year, after my fill of conversation and turkey, I plan to take my secret napping habit out of the closet and onto the couch. My guests may giggle nervously, even whisper a comment... but more likely, they'll grab a pillow and join me.

Discover Your Own Pearls

When was the last time you took a nap? Yesterday, or years ago? If it's been a long time, is it because you simply don't need that midday break, or that you won't let yourself have it? If the latter, choose a day this week to allow yourself a 10-15 minute nap. See what resistant or happily indulged feelings come up. Take a step towards slowing down your busy day...

THOSE HOLIDAY CARDS

"Everything you do can be done better from a place of relaxation."
— Stephen C. Paul

I almost canceled our walk, my friend told me as we picked up the pace through the neighborhood with our dogs. With the holiday season here, she continued, there's just too much to get done. Shopping, cooking, cleaning. Plus, I haven't even started my Christmas cards!

Why don't you just skip them this year, I suggested? She looked at me like I had just spoken in a different language, one difficult for her to comprehend. Skip them, she said? Why, that's impossible. Everyone is expecting me to do them. Ever since we started doing these elaborate photoshopped cards, my friends and family look forward to seeing the latest creation. I enjoy it, she slowly added, but then again...

With that, her voice trailed off into the wind.

The holiday card, touted as a missive of good cheer, can be anything but. Just what did people think of writing holiday cards, I wondered? It seems that underneath the cheeriest of greetings can be found the most cynical of attitudes...

Why do you send them, I asked another friend? Well, you never know when you might need a place to stay, she joked. Hoping to cajole more positive thoughts, I continued. And what do you like most about doing them? She thought for a moment, then sarcastically said what she liked most was finishing them and dropping them off at the post office. Least? Getting started.

Sigh.

It seems some people approach the idea of writing a card with as much enthusiasm as eating a five-pound fruitcake. It appears overwhelming and likely to make them queasy. One woman deals with this by keeping the cards she plans to write in a special place — untouched in the basement. She keeps meaning to fill them out, she says.

Whether writing or receiving, everyone has their opinions. People told me boo to cards with no photo and no personal signature, yeah to cards with Kodak stamped on the back; boo to form letters that brag, yeah to newsy, brightly written pieces. Bragging in particular seemed to irk people. Just because little Emily can translate five different languages at age 7, they say, doesn't mean anyone wants to hear about it. As one friend said, "Everyone knows your life is not perfect, so it's okay to say so in your Christmas letter!"

With all that, I began wondering why anyone writes Christmas cards at all. As I sat getting my hair trimmed the other day, I asked my hairdresser why he wrote cards. In the corner of my eye I could see the big "Merry Christmas" banner in the waiting room and the tree twinkling with lights. Why, it's one of my favorite parts of the holiday, he said. For him, the cards are part of the reassuring ritual of the holiday season. He plays Christmas carols, makes old-fashioned ice-box cookies and sits down to pen personal notes, thinking fondly of each person as he seals the envelope. When he receives cards, he tapes them to the frame of the bay windows in his kitchen, feeling grateful for all the friends and family in his life. He carves out time and cherishes every moment.

Others have different methods of finding enjoyment in this ritual. Rather than add it as another item on their busy holiday list, one couple I know sends out Christmas cards in July. That way, they can lie by the pool and luxuriate in the writing. The cards arrived stamped with the message, "Way ahead of the crowd." And they are.

Another friend has made a party of it, literally. "I invite a few friends over every year to sit around and eat, drink, chat and get our cards done," says my friend Carla. "It's always been lots of fun." By the end of the evening, guests go home not only with a passel of cards, but treasured memories as well.

To me, that's the way to go. Pass the pretzels and the pens. The party favor at the end of the evening is a stack of completed cards.

Speaking of which, I haven't done mine this year. And I'm not going to feel guilty about it, either. Should a wave of inspiration hit (or an invitation to a card-writing party), I just may change my mind. But in case I don't, I've got a back-up plan. A way to send good cheer and heartfelt gratitude to all my friends, family and even people I've never met, but I bet I'd like.

It's called writing a book. Happy holidays!

Discover Your Own Pearls

When the holidays roll around, do you dread writing cards? How can you either make it more enjoyable or — without guilt — decide to pass this year? Make your plan now...

JOY

"For happiness one needs security, but joy can spring like a flower even from the cliffs of despair."
— Ann Morrow Lindbergh

For a moment, I thought I hadn't heard right. "I'm just riding the crest of a wave," my father said. "Life just keeps getting better and better and I don't know when it will peak. I feel such joy."

Joy? My father? I could see it if he was in a Tuscany villa eating caviar, but that was far from the situation. Instead, he was living hundreds of miles away in the house we had recently moved out of, which by now was stripped of all furniture and even without electricity. His health wasn't great and his finances even worse. It was a couple of weeks before Christmas and no stockings were hung by his chimney. It was as if the Grinch had visited and taken every morsel, save for a folding chair and cot. So… joy?

It was then that I started pondering joy. You hear all about it during the holidays. The speakers in the mall jewelry shop pipe in "Joy to the World" as you peruse necklaces. Charity ads extol the joy of giving. And holiday cards arrive in small metal mailboxes urging the reader to have a joyful holiday.

But when I looked around, I saw fewer people in what appeared to be joy and more in frustration, indifference or numbness. Yet everyone seemed to be searching for it, this elusive joy. Could it be found in the taste of rum balls slipping down our throat? Or caroling on a brisk night? Certainly joy would be nestled under the covers with our children?

My own discovery was that joy was none of these places... and all of them. Whereas your garden variety happiness is tied to events — you get a promotion, you're happy — joy exists regardless of circumstances. You can find joy in rush hour traffic or while sweeping the floor because, as Eckhart Tolle writes, "Pleasure is always derived from something outside you, whereas joy arises from within."

The only reason that we're not drooling with rapture 24 hours a day is that we've buried it. Joy is crushed underneath a hundred packages and rushed by as we think about upcoming parties and obligations. But when we pause and breathe in the pine-scented, deeply felt gratitude of the moment, it arrives. Sometimes it comes on a sleigh of laughter; other times a tender ache sweet as a snowflake.

It has been said that Michelangelo could "see" his sculptures hidden in a chunk of marble before he started. His job, he said, was simply to cut away the excess and bring forth the beauty imprisoned inside. Joy is like that. It's always inside us, but often obscured by layers of fear, expectation, worry, rushing. As Jack Kornfield writes, "We do not have to improve ourselves; we just have to let go of what blocks our heart (to find joy)."

Last week, joy seemed like it was miles away. We had bought a puppy and everyone had fallen in love, but we were fearful of having to return him because of allergic reactions from my daughters. Also, while trying to juggle holiday decorating, I was chasing after our new four-legged roommate, who was busy inscribing teeth marks on the underbelly of pink flip-flops.

As the week wore on, I grew more despondent, telling myself the story that I was miserable because of the events in my life. As I sat down to write, all of a sudden I remembered. Joy comes from within, regardless of circumstance. I had conned myself into believing that I wouldn't feel happy until the "puppy situation" was solved. But the beauty of joy is that it can appear in an instant if you let it. No life events need to change. Suddenly I was flooded with peace as I released my worries, my fears, my need to have a solution. I relaxed into the moment. I wasn't in "joy," but I was pretty darn near it.

A few hours later, I was out walking when what had eluded me for weeks came full force. My heart burst open like a ripe plum. I felt filled up and satiated at the deepest level of my being, full of aching tenderness and joy so deep that it overflowed in tears. Nothing in my life had changed to bring on such bliss. It was exactly as it was 5 minutes earlier. But this time, I was ready to open to what had been there all along.

On Christmas morning, if I get lost in heaps of wrapping paper and cornbread stuffing, I'll think of my Dad. He wasn't blinded by the illusion of joy "out there." He knew it was inside and always available. The challenge was letting go of what stood between him and his joy. In that empty house, he did just that... and found it everywhere.

Discover Your Own Pearls

What stories have you been telling yourself about why you're not feeling joyful? What outside events have you been blaming for your mood? Lack of money? Ill health? A broken fingernail? List all of them... and let them go, at least for a few minutes. You can retrieve your worries later. But for now, breathe for a few moments and open to the joy that's the essence of who you are...

HOLIDAY HANGOVERS

"The darkness looks more comforting to us than the natural radiance of our being. We seek solace in comfort and entertainment, in sneaking away to veg out in front of the television. Instead, we can look at what we have and strengthen our inspiration."
— Sakyong Mipham Rinpoche

As I sit here licking the crumbs off the last holiday sugar cookie, I sigh. It tastes so good. Okay, two cookies ago it tasted good; now, it's kinda lost its flavor. But better to polish them off today, I rationalize, than leave them around for the New Year. I'll take my pleasures now, leave the paying up for later.

I get up, still wearing sweatpants from this morning, and look out the window. It's a beautiful afternoon, mid-seventies. I regret that I didn't get out for a walk. I realize I'm still in the holiday fog — hung over from too much food, too much spending, not enough mindfulness.

When I get in this mode, comfort and pleasure are my mantra. Wanna try that piece of fudge? Sure, why not! How about a magazine? And why exercise when that recliner is calling my name?

So what, you may say. What's wrong with a little pleasure? The problem isn't comforting ourselves — a cookie here, a frivolous purchase there. It's when we start focusing more and more on something outside ourselves to make us feel good. Then we keep repeating the same formula, even though it's not satisfying. As author Stephen Levine says, "Pleasure is… a temporary gratification of desire. Happiness is a deeper satisfaction, a feeling of wholeness, of non-neediness."

Like a Doberman running after a ball, when chasing pleasure, everything else fades but the object of our desire.

I sigh again, then crack open the window. Immediately a rush of moist, leafy air comes through. I feel spaces opening inside myself. It feels good.

I remember the words of Pema Chodron. "When there's so much space, why do we keep putting on dark glasses, putting in earplugs and covering ourselves with armor?" she asks. When we find ourselves caught in cravings, she suggests that "At your own speed, starting where you are, you begin to open the door and the windows." It's not about changing our lives on January 1. It's a gentle process, releasing cravings one at a time, that leads us from more mindless pleasure to wide-open happiness.

I absent-mindedly pick up a potato chip, and a slant of awareness comes in. I stop and breathe for a moment. I reach in further. How do I feel? Is this what I want? No, it's not. I'm feeling a little blue. I want to lie on the grass and look at the clouds.

An hour later, I'm fixated on my desire to get the house clean. I'm distracted, enjoying nothing. I catch myself and check in again, cracking the window a bit wider. Is this what I want? I decide instead to rest for five minutes, then am able to continue cleaning with a lighter step, fully appreciating the smell of wax on wood, the pungent snap of ammonia streaming onto tile.

One moment at a time, I check in rather than check out. I start reconnecting with the wisdom and strength inside me, rather than reaching for a rote pleasure outside of me.

Sometimes awareness doesn't kick in until after I've eaten the cookie or picked up the People magazine. But that's okay. As I start this year, the window's cracking open wider and wider. And the view? Limitless.

Discover Your Own Pearls

Everyone has those times when we feel vibrantly alive, as well as those when we get into behaviors that numb us. It can be overeating, overdrinking, drugs, too much shopping, too much working — the list goes on and on. Which do you lean towards when you're not feeling able to fully open to your light? What could you do instead? This week, just observe. Open the window, just a crack...

WHERE EVERYBODY KNOWS YOUR NAME

*"We are all longing to go home to some place we have never been —
a place half-remembered and half-envisioned we can only catch
glimpses of from time to time. Community. Somewhere, there are
people to whom we can speak with passion without having the words
catch in our throats. Somewhere a circle of hands will open to receive
us, eyes will light up as we enter, voices will celebrate with us
whenever we come into our own power. Community means strength
that joins our strength to do the work that needs to be done. Arms to
hold us when we falter. A circle of healing. A circle of friends."*
— Starhawk

Seems whenever I cook up a recipe for holiday cheer, life has its own ideas. This season was no exception. My version: shop early, bake cookies, see holiday lights, relax. Life's version: become a barista.

Considering that I haven't worked retail since my teens, and that my knowledge of coffee and cash registers is pretty shaky, I have to admit that this was a creative, unexpected twist. And to toss it in the midst of a busy holiday season was especially interesting, but timetables don't matter much to life.

My friends Sook and Allen Rasafar certainly would have preferred a different timetable. They had just opened a coffee shop — the culmination of a lifelong dream — when Sook fell off a high ladder, fracturing her neck and spine. In a moment, not only was their new business in jeopardy, but so was her life. I got the call late in the afternoon, after a day of watching my stress levels ricochet up and down as I navigated holiday bell ringers and "three-hours only!" sales. Sook is being airlifted to the hospital, Allen said. It looked bad.

I knew him well enough to know the unasked question. His wife and three daughters were his main concern, but the niggling worry would be how to keep the coffee shop doors open. So I chucked my holiday to-do list and showed up with an apron and reindeer antlers. I was ready to work.

When I arrived at the coffee shop, I heard the gentle snores of a man sleeping peacefully on the couch. Surprisingly, Allen looked happy about this. That's my badge of success, he said. He's paying us the highest compliment possible. The fact that he feels comfortable enough here to nap on the couch tells me we're slowing people down. They feel at home.

Well, that's unusual I thought. Certainly not the typical retail mentality. This type of pampering could lead to something radical, reflecting the words inside a silver-foil Christmas card I'd received the day before that urged, "Good will towards men." I wondered what else I'd find in this refreshing, comforting little place.

The next day, my friend Barb showed up ready to help out. Typically that would be the act of a long-time friend, but she'd only met them once. My father-in-law Charles also appeared, greeting customers as if they were old acquaintances. Patrons came in and asked about Sook, taking prayer requests back to their churches. Before long, people the Rasafars didn't even know were showing up with hot meals for their family and stuffing extra tips in the jar on their way out.

One man sat at a table doing newspaper crossword puzzles. He overheard Barb and I talking about needing cheerful decorations in the shop to offset Sook's tragedy. He slipped out and returned an hour later, arms full of large poinsettias. Those flowers were followed by a vase of fresh blooms offered by the army recruiters next door — the same ones who had dropped everything to drive Allen across town when Sook fell.

Before long, people were letting down their defenses. Tables of strangers were pulled together. Did anyone know a five-letter word for soup server, asked the man doing crossword puzzles? What about that icy weather ahead, asked another? While people outside were boldly vying for parking spots to finish up errands, inside time seemed to stop in the glow of the coffee shop. People slowed down enough to see each other. To hear each other. They shared their stories, breaking the ice inside even as it grew colder outside.

A few days later, Allen came in with relief all over his face. It was a miracle, he said. Even the doctors couldn't quite explain how someone that badly hurt would now not only walk, but possibly make a full recovery. People hugged and we all gave silent thanks.

The recovery was amazing, yet so was what I saw around me. Out of nothing, a community had formed. Old and young, pacifist and activist, Jew and Christian. Without judgment they connected, bound only by their humanity and interest in the welfare of another. As I watched, the old song from "Cheers" came into my head. "Making your way in the world today takes everything you've got. Taking a break from all your worries, sure would help a lot. Wouldn't you like to get away? Sometimes you want to go where everybody knows your name, and they're always glad you came."

Just then a retiree taking music lessons in his spare time started playing holiday tunes on the shop's organ. I figured I'd hear Christmas music this season, but I'd envisioned listening to it while scurrying through the mall. Life, happily, had other ideas.

Discover Your Own Pearls

Do you have a community to retreat to in your life? A place where people open their arms to you without judging? If not, what stops you from joining one? Or creating one? Write down your vision of what an ideal community would look like.

Strands of Pearls

GIRLFRIENDS

"A friend is someone who knows the song in your heart, and can sing it back to you when you have forgotten the words."
— Anonymous

Some women won't admit they color their hair. Others tiptoe around the fact that they're seeing a therapist, or that their last birthday wasn't, in fact, 29. But recently I've discovered a secret that far more women have in common... and far fewer reveal. A lack of friends.

Now, I'm not talking about social misfits, women who are clueless about how to have a conversation beyond hello. I'm talking about funny, warm, witty, talented, even sociable people. People like us.

When my family moved to Texas two years ago, I thought I was the only one around without friends — a situation I figured would be quickly rectified. I knew what I wanted — close friends like those I had left behind. Women I could share laughs with over cherry pie, women who weren't bored to hear the mundane details of my life, women I could call at 2 a.m. in an emergency. I flung myself upon the social scene, joining everything from fitness center to church, school committee to neighborhood bunco group.

It didn't take long to realize this would be no overnight job. In fact, finding friends felt like a job in itself. I'd scan a group for some signs of chemistry and instead feel the fizzle. I'd meet someone promising and join them for coffee, only to hear a an hour long monologue about their judgmental mother-in-law, ending with an enthusiastic "let's do it again!" Not.

Some were great intellectual conversationalists, but hung garlic up to keep away their feelings. Others were wonderful, but very, very busy. You can't grow a friendship on a 30 minute lunch twice a year. One woman seemed perfect — until her kids came over to visit and terrorized my kids, carpet, pantry and glass vase all within the first hour.

It felt like a tennis volley that never got anywhere. I'd send the ball whizzing enthusiastically over the net, and they'd let it drop and go shopping. Or they'd send one over, and I'd sidestep it. I was waiting for those partners who could volley back and forth, from shared interest to spontaneous glee, taking the game farther and deeper.

One day I was on a party barge with a group of acquaintances and finally found the nerve to declare my frustration. I stuttered out that making friends seemed easy when I was younger, but that making deep connections seemed harder nowadays.

There was a silence — I figured they were all planning an escape route — and then another woman said, "Me too." Pretty soon everyone was confessing. Was it that we weren't school kids anymore? Or that since we were older, we'd all experienced powerful friendships and now the bar was too high? Perhaps we were so busy trying to keep up with our fast paced lives that friendships were the casualty? That no one has the time or patience for the slow tending to a friendship?

Of course, it always seems like everyone else has gobs of friends, because they're busy dropping mentions of "trips to the lake with friends" or "that funky party the other night..." What they don't mention, perhaps don't even realize themselves, is that there are friends and there are FRIENDS.

The difference is between a Big Mac, which is satisfying in it's own time and place, and a filet mignon. Or, as Kathleen A. Brehony muses in her book Living a Connected Life, "So why do we have just a single word for friend? Why do we expect one word to describe relationships as distinct as someone we play tennis with occasionally to another we would die for and whose presence in our life gives meaning, love and rich emotional experiences?"

On the barge that day, we all admitted we had plenty of the former — the mom we exchange pleasantries with waiting for the bus, the co-worker with whom you discuss sports in the hall. We appreciate them. But we never seem to have enough of those friends who reflect to us our best selves, who sacrifice for us and we for them, who are comfortable enough to raid our refrigerator without asking. When we want to tell someone that we woke up and found the most beautiful butterfly looking in the window at us, we find our address books are jammed full... but there are few we can actually call.

I certainly don't have all the answers. But perhaps the five minutes we could have spent dusting may be better spent calling a friend to see what miniscule event brightened her day. We could take a small step and admit that our hair isn't naturally blonde. Then we could take the bigger step and reveal what far too many hide — that we need each other.

Discover Your Own Pearls

Make a list of your friends and see which category they fit in — friends you can call at 2 a.m. in an emergency and "the rest." Are you happy with that balance? If not, look at what might be getting in the way of forming the kind of friendships you want. Visualize the ideal friend for you. Then, make a commitment to spending more time deepening the friendships you already have or meeting new people who might be a better match.

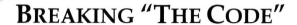

BREAKING "THE CODE"

"Fear makes strangers of people who would be friends."
— Shirley Maclaine

B y the end of the hour-long hike, I didn't know her last name. Or even what she had for breakfast that day. But I did know that she was Jewish, liked dogs and that she was pregnant with a daughter whose disease might take her life before she was ever born.

She was vulnerable enough to speak about something that mattered to her, despite the fact that she barely knew me, and I was open enough to listen deeply.

In other words, we broke The Code.

You know, the one that says no more than a smile and a few awkward lines are required when coming across people you don't know. It's also the one that says if you do decide to talk, start with the kids and maybe move to weather. And whatever you do, stay in your head, not in your heart.

The Code is everywhere. When I first joined a gym, I bounced in the door ready for some bicep and friendship building. Instead, I ran smack dab into The Code. Unless you came with an old friend, you weren't supposed to talk to one another. It didn't matter if a person was exercising just 30 inches away from you. You minded your own business. If you tried to talk, you'd be met with a polite answer, and then silence again. After you'd seen someone about, oh, 50 times, then you could warm up your vocal cords instead of just your body.

However, one day the gym Code shattered. There was a woman I had seen there and even casually chatted with about schools a few times. But one morning she came through the door in a walker. She had been at a ranch when suddenly she lost the use of her legs. The doctors weren't sure if she would ever regain their full use again. It was Christmas time, and I still remember a forlorn sprig of holly hung from her walker. The few of us who were there encircled her, talking and crying, breaking The Code with our bare hearts.

But I'd rather not wait for a medical calamity to connect with someone. I'd rather have deep connections strung together like Christmas lights throughout my weeks — connections of joy and sorrow, of philosophical meanderings and dreams, of laughter and surprise. Connections with strangers, connections with good friends.

When I lived in Phoenix, I was pals for 15 minutes each month with the short, bespectacled "bug guy" who came and sprayed our house. By breaking The Code that you don't get to know people who do services for you, I learned about his love of old movies, and how he and his wife were trying to earn enough money to start a vintage movie rental shop on the outskirts of town. The Thursday pool guy really wanted a business degree and was working three jobs to save up for it. The mail carrier, who I knew loved color and design, spotted the off-color hues we were painting our house and cared enough to point it out and offer suggestions before delivering a package next door.

It's all about dropping your agenda, dropping your assumptions, dropping your distracting mind chatter and instead being there, in the moment, with full attention on another human being. It's about daring to open ourselves to another. And about creating space for a connection that just might touch your heart, get you to think, or surprise you with a snort of laughter. But when we're so focused on checking things off on our to-do lists, racing from one thing to another with a pragmatic end in mind, we don't leave room for the magic that can happen in an instant between two people.

Just this morning, I volunteered at my daughter's field day events at school, watching moms silently conform to The Code as they waited to be told where to help out. Yet when I started talking with them, the relief was palpable. It ended up one just moved here and was feeling isolated and homesick. The gratitude she showed me for taking the time to ask about what she needed and how she was adjusting was a huge gift to me. Certainly not what I expected when I walked over this morning.

Some days I'm not up for breaking The Code. I'd rather stay in my safe, secure shell and remain anonymous. Or put on my too-comfortable social mask and not dig any deeper. That's okay, too. Nothing is lost on those days. But then again, nothing is gained, either.

Discover Your Own Pearls

How many times this week have you reached out to someone you don't know, even if it's just a smile? If you haven't, what's stopping you? What are your hesitations? And if you don't feel you have anything to gain from a connection with a stranger, or with deepening a relationship with an acquaintance, that's something to ponder, too.

RECIPE FOR HEALING

"Let your food be your medicine and let your medicine be your food."
— Hippocrates

Every evening they arrive, ringing the doorbell while shuffling hot casseroles, lopsided cakes and salad greens bouncing in Tupperware containers. The door opens and hellos are exchanged, a shoulder is squeezed and then warm bread and fresh tomatoes are passed from hand to hand before they leave. Sharon closes the door, a full dinner for four and small plant now filling her table, and she sighs with gratitude. A miracle has just happened, and she knows it.

When Sharon got breast cancer, she wasn't sure how exactly she would get through. With two always-hungry teenage boys and a husband who was overextended himself, she knew she'd need healthy meals, yet the rounds of chemotherapy often left her too exhausted to walk around much, let alone cook. That's when the food started arriving. Not the kind handed to you through the car window with the blurry sound of speakers confirming the order. Not the kind pre-made and wrapped in plastic at the grocery store. And not the kind frozen, then microwaved for five minutes before being scarfed down from a partitioned plate.

It was the kind made from scratch that arrives without strings, other than perhaps those used to tie a cake box. It was the kind that heals.

After my father died, such a gift arrived at my door. My

friend Meeta came with a big hug and containers filled with homemade Indian delicacies. Every time I took a bite of those plump samosas, I could feel my father stroking my forehead, telling me it was going to be all right. It took me right back to childhood and autumn nights when I lay in bed sick, watching the door gently open and my mother come in bearing bowls of Greek chicken soup and a cool compress. There was something so nurturing about getting food from someone who clearly cared, someone who put your well-being above their convenience.

"The Buddha said that when we offer someone food, we're not just giving that person something to eat; we're giving far more," says author Sharon Salzberg. "We're giving them strength, health, beauty and clarity of mind, even life itself, because none of those things is possible without food. We're offering the stuff of life itself." A miracle, indeed.

In addition, cooking for others is a sacrifice of what has become our most valuable resource — time. During the period it takes to plan the meal, search out ingredients, cook, wrap and deliver it... well, in that space of time you could have finished that last bit of income taxes, returned a couple of calls and perhaps even sat down for a bite to eat yourself.

In Sharon's case, her friend Tracy juggles a list of 28 neighbors, PTA members and band boosters who take turns preparing and delivering meals. "People want to do something to help, and making a meal is something they can do," Tracy says. "Not everyone can go with Sharon when she has her infusion because they have other things to do. But everyone can make a meal."

We all want to wave a magic wand and cure people of their ills or the grief of loss, but that kind of magic exists only in storybooks. We have another kind. Mix a few eggs, butter and flour with a heart that wants to reach out to another and you've created a powerful recipe — and one whose effects will linger on long after the last biscuit is eaten...

Discover Your Own Pearls

Think of someone you know who isn't feeling their best, whether from grief, the flu, depression or just the blahs. Consider offering them a small chunk of your time by cooking and delivering something. It can be anything from an entire meal to a plate of sugar cookies. It doesn't have to be gourmet, just made with love.

GIFTS FROM THE HEART

"When we die, all that we take with us
is that which we have given away."
— Robert Gard

B uying gifts was always like target practice for me — the
faster I hit the mark, the better. Take toys, for instance.
There was no dawdling along the aisles, looking
through kaleidoscopes or squeezing baby dolls to hear
them burp. Instead, I quickly scanned shelves for bargains
while veering my cart around errant toddlers, then found the
quickest escape route, bypassing the chatty cashiers for the
nimble-fingered one just promoted to management. In and out
in ten minutes.

That was exactly how I had found the matching
blanket/doll set for the sleepover birthday party my 8-year-
old daughter Chloe would be attending. By the day of the
party, I had it wrapped in purple paper with a generic card
tacked on.

But that morning, as she came into the kitchen for
breakfast, Chloe had other ideas. In her hand she cradled a
small brown box, proudly whispering that inside was an even
more suitable gift for the party.

She set her tiny box in the shadows of the giant cereal
boxes on the table, took off the lid and showed me the
contents — a lipstick-sized horse with a pink glitter saddle,
some favorite rocks from her collection, a "diva" charm and a

137

pint-sized pencil that she had painstakingly sharpened until it was a one-inch stub with an eraser on the end.

I sat and stared at the box, and was utterly surprised at my own reaction. Instead of cooing, I spat. What! I said. How can you give away these things? Isn't this the charm Granny gave you? And didn't you spend the last of your vacation allowance to buy these rocks? Isn't that your favorite horse! Besides, I've already bought a gift!

Of course, remorse quickly followed, and just as quickly came the unsettling realization that somewhere in me, I believed in scarcity. That there wasn't enough to go around. That letting something go was the same as losing out.

These beliefs were reflected in our respective gift searches. Chloe had blissfully prepared her gifts as a sacrament to the altar of friendship. She had spent the morning going through tucked away heart-shaped boxes and dresser-top displays to find those things that tickled her heart. Since what we give is what we get, she had wrapped her day in good feelings; mine was wrapped in joyless expediency. She let go, I clung.

To children, heart-felt giving is as natural as breathing. I still remember when Chloe's red-haired friend William came to visit. He had a gift carefully wrapped up in pink tissue paper. Inside was a fuzzy tennis ball with grass stains on it (for our yellow lab) and strawberry flavored lipstick that had obviously been tested more than a time or two. No matter. His cheeks flushed red as his hair with the joy of giving the gift, and Chloe's did too upon receiving it.

Children aren't afraid to give because they trust in the flow of good through the universe. They trust in the sun warming their feet after the rain clouds go away, in teddy bears that grin at you night after night, in a benevolent world that cracks wide open to show you its riches. In gifts that can be given, but not given away.

As I pondered this, I remembered a story I'd heard recently of an old Asian man who came to a local hospital and handed over a crumpled envelope stuffed with $1,000. When asked for explanation, he said that his wife had died there a year ago to the day. He had since sold her belongings and wanted to honor her by donating the proceeds to the hospital.

I could just imagine him, in his grief after her death, tenderly holding a string of her pearls in his hands, gently folding a favorite sweater. And I could see the tiniest of smiles play across his lips as he thought of how that old hat she wore to the theater, those worn gloves, would now go to helping buy crutches or medicine for a needy child. Despite his pain, he would go on and heal because he hit the mark we so often miss. He knew that what we hold in our heart always outweighs what we hold in our hands.

Discover Your Own Pearls

When was the last time you gave something away? It could be money you donated to a charity, tithing at a church, or a favorite sweater that a friend admired so you handed it over. How hard or easy was this for you to do? What stops you from doing more? How might you benefit from doing more? Find someone you admire with a giving attitude and see what you can learn from them — and at the same time acknowledge yourself for all you have given through your lifetime.

HOLLYWOOD LOVE

"True love comes quietly, without banners or flashing lights.
If you hear bells, get your ears checked."
— Erich Segal

Some wives get giddy with gladiolas. Or Lammes chocolate-covered strawberries. Or a sonnet tucked under their pillow. But me, I'm easy. All my husband has to do to make my heart sing is dry the dishes...

When Charley and I first started dating, we valued the more traditional, Hollywood-approved signs of love. We had impromptu picnics in the park and held hands in cafés, earnestly discussing our dreams and fears. Flowers arrived regularly, along with boxes of marzipan chocolates.

Eventually, these coltish signs of affection turned into a more solid love, leading to marriage, two daughters, a house and all the responsibilities that come with that. Our lives changed — became busier, fuller and wonderful in different ways. But as time went by, I began to think that things weren't... enough. The messages were all around me. Women were swooning over diamonds on TV, having passionate trysts in movies, going on exotic vacations in magazine articles. We weren't. For us, weeks went by when daily tasks left us little time to talk, let alone prepare rose petal-strewn baths.

So, I decided we needed "improvement." I began making lists of how we could upgrade our marriage. Perhaps we could read love poems together in a back yard tent lit with candles? Or have soul-searching conversations as we walked along Town Lake? All I knew was that I had an expectation, and it wasn't being met.

And then one evening, late, as I was sitting alone in bed looking through a folder of "interesting date ideas" — trying to decide between scuba diving lessons and laser tag — I heard a thunking noise coming from the kitchen. I walked in and found Charley, bone-tired after a long day, drying and putting away dinner dishes.

Now let me clarify one thing. Charley likes a neat workbench, but couldn't care less if the kitchen counter has that uncluttered, Zen-like flow to it. I'm the one who values that. As I watched him rub his eyes, then slowly reach for a spatula before plunking it in the drawer, it came to me. He wasn't doing this for himself, he was doing this because he loved me. Loved me enough to want to see my burdens lifted. Loved me enough to sacrifice his own needs, as it was obvious he'd rather be stretched out in bed. Loved me enough to do this without boasting, without complaining, but as a heartfelt gesture of affection.

Suddenly I realized that signs of his love had been all around me — I just hadn't seen them. Instead of being cloaked in rubies and romantic songs, they were subtly dressed in domestic disguise. Instead of an annual grand gesture loud enough to dent our bank account, he showed his feelings through simple daily gifts of time and thought.

Once I took off my Hallmark-colored glasses, I began to see all the ways he loved me — shall I count them? More precious than scented love letters, he leaves MapQuest directions on my car seat before I set out for a new destination. He lets me sleep in on weekends, watching the girls and tenderly placing a blanket under the door to cut down on noise. Instead of puttering in the garage, he fixes my aching, broken... computer. He even slays spiders for me. What more could a woman want?

Of course, what you focus on grows. When I focused on the lack in our marriage, the lack grew. And once I started focusing on the small, affectionate miracles of our daily lives, they grew, too. It became a give and take, a wonderful dance between us of a foot massage here, a closet organized there. Each loving act — seen and fully appreciated — fueled more. Embers turned to fire.

Now I'm not saying that I'd turn down a hand-drawn Jacuzzi bath, complete with candles and lavender oils, if it's offered. But that's not what really makes me feel loved. It's when Charley sneaks in afterwards with a bottle of 409 and cleans out the tub — now that's love.

Discover Your Own Pearls

Observe all the "not so obvious" ways you and your partner express love for each other. Think about what he's communicating to you when he bathes the children, spends time talking to the in-laws, or takes out the trash. Can you appreciate his unique way of showing his love?

TAKE FIVE

"Rituals are formulas by which harmony is restored."
— Terry Tempest Williams

It all started when our girls were young, on one of those days when my husband Charley and I had spent more time putting out fires than sparking one of our own. When the laundry sat in piles along with the bills. When our communication had been reduced to a shorthand of to-do lists and grunts as we mopped milk puddles and bandaged knees.

At the end of the day, we waved our white flags and gratefully crawled into bed, our resources spent. As we flickered wan smiles at each other from opposite sides of the king-sized bed, we knew something had to change. Our connection was fading.

So, we devised a quickie — of the non-physical variety. In desperation to get below the surface with each other quickly, we began the "5-minute ritual." We decided that every night, we'd each tell the other the high and low points of our day, followed by something we appreciated about each other and our intention for the next day.

The acorn of that simple ritual has grown into the oak we lean on today. Perhaps it's a day I'm especially ragged, yet Charley telling me how he admires the way I handled a situation or how my eyes still intrigue him is just enough to lift me. On the days when discussions are mired in the ozone of foggy thinking, we get a breath of fresh air when he shares a vulnerable moment with the kids. For five minutes, we get real. And those moments, shared over days, months and years, turn a small daily investment into a wealth of connected riches.

We've tried 5-minute rituals in other areas of our lives, too, from mealtime prayers to after-school touch points. At bedtime, Chloe gets a chance to reflect on her day with three things she's grateful for. We both get to mentally play with those things she loves, which have included cheese crisps, her big sister, marbles, and bubble mountains in the tub. As she drifts off to sleep, those images float past the border and mingle with her dreams.

Alix and I read a book passage every night. We bypass the trivial and get right to the meat. Now, we are reading "Don't Sweat the Small Stuff for Teens." In five minutes, we jump into everything from "mental aikido" for diffusing arguments to making peace with your mistakes. The serious is then lightened up with a 10 second "squishy" from dad — a playful, giggle-infused hug.

I take five for myself, too. I grab a journal for at least five minutes a day — more if I connect with time and inspiration — and tune into my mind and body at that exact moment. It's fascinating to observe that 5-minute snapshot changing day to day.

Sometimes I take advantage of idle time and use it to find a moment of connection. While waiting in the grocery line, I try to stem irritation by sending heartfelt, positive thoughts to those around me — including the elderly woman in front of me slowly extracting coins from her wallet... penny by penny. And of course, being a devotee of the power of ritual in concise chunks of time, I see the mandated moment of silence in schools as an opportunity waiting to happen with possibilities for prayers, meditations or emotional check-ins.

It's so easy to get overwhelmed with all we want to do, from getting the dinner pans scoured to instilling character in our kids. We say we want more meaning in our lives, then get swept away by trivialities. We can't save the world. We can't even save our peace of mind some days. But surely we can start... five minutes at a time.

Discover Your Own Pearls

We all already have daily rituals — pouring our morning coffee followed by reading the paper, brushing our teeth right before putting on our clothes, reading a child a bedtime story. Why not be a bit more selective and trade out some rituals that give you little payback for those that offer more bang for your buck? What are a few things you could do daily for five minutes — alone or with someone — that could really make a difference?

THE ENDANGERED DINNER PARTY

*"I am thankful for the mess to clean after a party because
it means I have been surrounded by friends."*
— Nancie J. Carmody

Perhaps it's the name that scares me. Dinner party. Right off, it presents a double whammy. There's "dinner," as in shopping, cooking, cleaning. Then there's "party," as in multiplying all of the above by more people, then adding the potential for unforeseeable mishaps — such as your newly skunked dog walking in the house or forgetting to mix sugar into the cake batter.

Most people I know would rather attempt to climb Mount Everest than throw a dinner party.

I certainly understand the reluctance. The trek can be hard. First, there's the food. My family's standby of bottled pasta sauce on top of dried-out spaghetti found in the back of the pantry just doesn't cut it. Nor do Oreos for dessert. So that means pulling out the cookbook and trying something new, which means setting myself up for much potential embarrassment. Luckily, my friends are prone to charitable lying. More candid acquaintances can meet me for lunch… at a restaurant.

Housekeeping is another matter. Just when you think the house is perfect, you notice that the toilet is clogged. As you're running past the door, disinfectant and grungy toilet brush in hand, the doorbell rings. The guests have arrived.

Before any of this, everyone must sift through their avalanche of activities to find a common date. And who to invite? It's easy when you have a group of friends who know each other and meet regularly. But often we're venturing into new territory, mixing people like chemistry solutions to see who will gel and who will blow up when combined. Or you invite someone you adore, but find that their spouse's favorite subject starts with the letter "m," as in me, me, me, me. While you're dropping every hint that the party is over — yawning, stretching, exclaiming how early you have to get up the next morning — they're oblivious. Even the dog gets it and heads to his crate.

So why bother? Why not just stay at base camp and see dinner parties as an unobtainable summit? After all, aren't they too complicated to fit into our busy, practical lives? Too intimate for our drive-by friendships where we connect only at the soccer game or office?

Many people don't ever bother. But they're the ones who have never seen the view from the summit. They don't know the easy flow of a group of friends who come over and crack open shellfish as easily as their defenses. By the flickering candlelight, these friends are comfortable with everything from tales of being the unlucky nerd in 7th grade to teasing debates on politics. Laughter mixes with the tangy tomatoes; warmth flows through the ovens and between guests. Like Lucy and Ricky, Fred and Ethel, old friends grow more intimate, putting feet up on couches, sharing private jokes, communicating without words.

Mixes of new couples have their own magic, too. A husband finds his friend's wife loves Irish poetry, too. As they gab by the bookshelves, others are savoring peach cobbler and the last bit of a tale recounting a near-death experience on the Himalayan mountains. Sparks fly. Stories melt in your mouth. Nothing is barred, nothing is judged. It's simply people breaking bread together.

So, when I stare up the mountain at my fears, I realize it's time to make the trek again. I've decided what's stopping me is wanting too much to be perfect — the food, the calendar, the house. Instead, I'm just going to begin. Make a Mexican chicken salad and let it be okay that I've forgotten the salt. Or worse yet, forgotten that the guests are vegetarians.

I'll invite people I like and release the rest. I'll leave shelves undusted, dog toys on the floor. I can aspire to candles and filet mignon, but if take-out pizza and a bare light bulb are all I can muster, that's okay, too. Because getting to the top isn't about the party, but the people. And suddenly you realize the top isn't towering Mount Everest, but a molehill as close as your living room.

Discover Your Own Pearls

When was the last time you had a dinner party — or, if that term seems too daunting, a "grub gathering?" What stops you from inviting people over? If you haven't entertained in months, or even years, decide if it's a conscious choice that you feel good about, or something you would like to do but avoid because of fears or perceived obstacles. Come up with some solutions, then take an imperfect jump and pick up the phone...

DADDY'S GIRLS

"There came to port last Sunday night the queerest little craft, without an inch of rigging on; I looked and looked - and laughed. It seemed so curious that she should cross the unknown water, and moor herself within my room - my daughter! O my daughter!"
— George Washington Cable

When he was young and single, my husband Charley daydreamed about being surrounded by women. Blondes, brunettes, a whole gaggle of babes. He was the hero, the apple of their adoring eyes.

And then his wish came true. He's surrounded all right... only these babes call him "dad."

He has fathered no sons, only girls. Which means that in almost any situation, he's outnumbered and trying to find his way through foreign territory.

For instance, his side of the bathroom sink is spare with a toothbrush and shaving cream. Stealthily advancing from the flank and into his domain are stray earrings and lipstick tubes. He could take his toothbrush and retreat to another bathroom, but those are occupied by the girls. Entering this territory is dangerous indeed, with its whirring blow-dryers and scents of pink bubblegum perfume. Worst of all, if he enters when someone is exiting, he may get hit with what any dad of daughters understands as "TMI," or "too much information." Things happen to daughters and wives in bathrooms that guys would rather not know about.

Sometimes they don't have a choice. Like when there's an "emergency" and they're drafted into duty, marched out the door to the nearest Walgreen's where they're asked to decipher something they find more complicated than the installation directions on their stereo system. Searching up and down the "feminine protection" aisle, they scan about 150 different products, each with different diagrams and descriptions. They stand there embarrassed, cell phone on ear, muttering if we women want wings or not? Overnight? Extra long or thin? And why the heck doesn't one size fit all?

Then there are sports. Charley used to play football. Even today, the smell of dank locker rooms and freshly mown turf puts a dreamy smile on his face. When our daughter Chloe was younger, he encouraged her to try soccer. Problem was, to her the thrill of the game wasn't in kicking the ball, but having the cutest uniform. I still remember her soccer practice in first grade when she wore a large pink tutu underneath her oversized jersey. With each kick, a flash of pink showed along with her smile. Dad watched sheepishly from the sidelines and finally let her quit when the coach wouldn't let the jersey go pink, too.

Sometimes, Charley tries to meet our daughters on their turf. Last week he magnanimously offered to take our high school daughter shopping for new frames for her glasses. She was looking for something to define her style, something innovative and unusual. So they drove in his pickup truck to… Costco! After arriving, Charley couldn't understand why she wasn't happy with any of the reasonably priced, perfectly good frames that were highlighted underneath the warehouse's florescent lighting. Had she not called me with an S.O.S., they probably would have ended up at Great Clips getting $8 hair cuts to top it off.

Lest you think two daughters and a wife aren't an overwhelming amount of estrogen for one man, consider this. Our ranks swell when female friends visit; little boys rarely venture into our house. Many of our friends also have daughters. When they visit, the wives yak and the younger girls run around like giggling banshees while the men huddle defensively around the barbecue pit, like pioneers of old circling the wagons for protection.

Here, these dads of daughters welcome the respite of simple talk. They don't have to puzzle out the intricacies of schoolyard friendships and whose best friend is now their worst enemy. They don't have to solve clothing crises or do heavy emotional lifting. They're safe at base camp, like they were back in their single days before the women invaded.

But if they stayed at the barbecue pit and never returned to the world of little girls, they'd also be "safe" from having their heart tied in a blissful little pink knot. They'd be "safe" from having a little girl bring them a broken toy and look at them as heroes when it's magically returned in one piece. They'd be safe from a pint-sized ballerina proposing to them over chocolate ice cream cones.

They're surrounded all right — by a lot of love, admiration and cast-off Barbie clothes. Well, my husband says, two out of three isn't bad.

Discover Your Own Pearls

If you're a dad with a daughter, when does living with her feel like foreign territory? Do you enjoy the humor and adventure in the differences, or are you (or her) always trying to change the other? What things do you do where you can just relax and enjoy each others' company? Do you do them often enough?

RANDOM NOTES OF KINDNESS

"Writing notes can be one of life's purest pleasures, in which the truly imaginative transmute the 'chore' into something special — the most basic form of communication, heart to heart."
— Catherine Calvert

Do you remember the thank-you notes that you wrote as a kid? Your mother chided you when you forgot, then sat you down, tersely pronouncing that Aunt Mildred would never send you another thing unless you thanked her. So, you dragged out your pen, glumly sat down, and eked out a few appropriate words. Just enough to satisfy your mother and Aunt Mildred. Chore done.

This is how I remember it, which didn't exactly inspire me to write letters. In addition, in order to write a letter, one actually has to track down the stationery, a workable pen, and stamps crushed somewhere between the telephone and address books in the kitchen drawer. The whole process can seem daunting, which means I often express thank-yous via email and over the phone. Or, regrettably, not at all.

But a note that appeared in my mailbox recently has started me thinking. Maybe I've been wrong…

My 5th grade daughter performed a short skit on the school announcements recently, and the very next day a letter arrived for her in the mail. Inside was a card congratulating her on a good performance. She read it and glowed with excitement, both from getting mail as well as a compliment.

Me, I was happy for her, and baffled. The person who had sent it was her teacher. Not her current one, but one from three years ago. The fact that it arrived the next day meant she had written it in the middle of a busy school day. With 20-odd students of her own this year, somehow this teacher had found not only the time to think about a former student, but the heart to do something totally unnecessary... and profoundly appreciated. I'd heard of random acts of kindness, but this was something new to me — a random "note" of kindness.

To understand this phenomena better, I called my friend Sandi. She is the ultimate note writer, keeping on hand a box with fun pens, stamps, nubby paper and blank note cards (so as not to be restricted to the Hallmark view of life). One day she'll send out a thank-you note, another an "I'm thinking about you" sentiment. Oddly enough, it brings her happiness. Sandi says she got this practice from her grandmother, who bought cards by the box and sent them to shut-ins, the bereaved and even those absent from her Sunday school class. In addition, she wrote to her grandkids every Sunday night. Every Tuesday, they received a treasured letter filled with the details of her life.

Some may argue that e-mail works just as well. It can be a great communication tool. But in "The Art of Thank You," writer Connie Leas says that "...an e-mailed note is too slap-dash. It lacks class, warmth, and generosity. It indicates that even though your impulse is to express your gratitude, you don't want to make much of an effort to do so. The recipient — however subliminally — is aware of this."

A hand-written letter, on the other hand, takes more time and effort. It also expresses itself more with the slant of the letters, the texture of the stationary, the chocolate stain at the bottom or a scent of perfume.

People rarely save printed emails, yet they do keep special boxes of letters. I know I do. Inside are love letters from my husband, notes of appreciation from readers, hand-made photography cards from relatives. Some of the most precious letters are from my now deceased parents. Holding them, I can trace their emotions in the curve of handwriting, read their thoughts as they flowed onto paper, rub my finger gently across "love, Dad" at the bottom. No e-mail has that power.

As I thought about all of this, I saw a blank note card sitting on my kitchen counter, earmarked for a friend whose husband had been seriously injured in Iraq. I'd been procrastinating on sending it, not sure what to say, not sure when I'd get by the post office. All excuses. So I sat down, imagined how she was feeling, and wrote from the heart. By the end of it, I was crying. In trying to touch her heart, I had touched my own. And suddenly I understood.

Writing cards isn't something we do because we have to. We do it because, just like a hefty package with ribbons and bows, we are giving a gift. We flow through pen onto page and travel the miles to offer an affectionate hug or playful ribbing. But before the "random note of kindness" has even left our mailbox, the gift has already arrived — to ourselves.

Discover Your Own Pearls

When was the last time you sent a letter or note to a friend? If it hasn't been recently, what gets in your way? Is it mind chatter like "I've nothing to say" or "I'm too busy"? Or perhaps it's too difficult to find the materials? Make it easy — put everything in a shoebox. Then, write one letter. You can even close your eyes and stick your finger in your address book and write to whoever pops up. Or, write to thank someone for something they'd never imagine. Perhaps the school librarian for lively story times. Or a neighbor for being available for your weekly walks. Just begin...

LET ME INTERRUPT YOU

"It can be amazing to hear what gifts come out of people's mouths
when you allow them to complete their thoughts
without interruption."
— Byron Katie

I plan to exercise today, my husband was saying, because... I know, I know, I said, because of that article we just read the other day that says exercising should be like brushing teeth. Something you do daily without even questioning. Right?

The icy stare told me that no, I was not right. As I was saying, he pointedly continued, I plan to exercise because I've been grouchy today and a bit down lately and realized that the endorphins would do me good.

I'd like to blame his annoyed response on the low endorphins, but I'm afraid it was my interruption that set him off. It's something I tend to do without noticing. Like blinking. Only no one glares at me when I blink...

Admittedly, sometimes I feel fully justified in interrupting others. When a salesman calls selling premium siding I don't need and is approaching his 83rd sentence without a breath as my soufflé is burning and doorbell is ringing... I finally jump in and interrupt him with a click.

Friends can be that way, too. I've sat through 30 minute monologues over coffee, waiting for the polite lapse in conversation that never comes. With those friends, the best plan is regular interruptions. I rationalize by calling that strategy.

I'm not the only one with interrupt-itis. At parties, they're as common as iced drinks. Stand in a small group that's talking animatedly and it's like playing in a quiz show. When a good topic is tossed out, people jump in as fast as possible, seeing who is first to "ding" the correct answer, which in this case is the witty retort or insightful comment. Ding just the right amount of times and you add bubble and life; too many, though, and the crowd moves elsewhere. Some people are so busy dinging that the conversation never reaches any depth; others ding so little that the mood becomes lethargic.

As I've started paying more attention to interrupting, it's been interesting to see when and why I do it, rather than just blurting out mindlessly. It seems there are endless reasons we interrupt. Sometimes we do it out of enthusiasm; other times because we're not really listening. It's used as a tool to change uncomfortable topics or assert conversational dominance.

Frequently, our interruptions come from a mind that's sped up and impatient. That's when we get in trouble. For instance, when people talk slowly, sometimes I have a hard time waiting for the conclusion. I figure I'll just help them along. It's kind of like scooting a toddler a little more quickly out the door. We reach the final destination faster... but only one of us is happy. And it's not the one scooted.

Likewise, some days I prefer to talk slowly, formulating the words at the exact moment that they're entering my mind, solving and creating as I speak. As I reach my climax, an interruption from someone is like a pinprick that deflates my whole thought process. My kids are especially adept at this. They sometimes slice my sentences so much that thoughts hiccup out bit by bit, the meaning lost long before the end.

Catching yourself interrupting and stopping yourself is especially hard with spouses. The longer the marriage, the worse the problem. My husband thinks he knows everything I'm going to say, and visa versa. So, we "help" each other out by finishing the others' sentences. But here's the catch. When I am able to repress my urge to interrupt him, waiting to see what he really planned to say, I'm often surprised. It's often not what I thought he'd say at all. That's pure delight. That's when I remember that if I really listen, there are always depths in others I'll find that I wouldn't have known about otherwise. No matter how well I know someone, stopping my own stream of thoughts to listen to theirs takes us a step closer.

Heck, science may one day prove that slowing down enough to listen may raise our level of feel-good endorphins. Perhaps that'll motivate us to stop interrupting... except when the siding salesman calls.

Discover Your Own Pearls

Start out by noticing when you interrupt others. Don't do anything. Just watch and look at the reason you're interrupting. Is it because you feel you can't get into the conversation otherwise? Are you trying to impress someone? Taking them for granted? After you've done this for a few days, try to catch yourself interrupting and stop yourself. Listen instead and see what happens.

MY LIFE AS A GROUPIE

"Call it a clan, call it a network, call it a tribe, call it a family.
Whatever you call it, whoever you are, you need one."
— Jane Howard

I'm a groupie. Luckily, my husband isn't jealous of the long hours I spend away from home. Perhaps that's because this obsession doesn't involve rock stars. Or music... usually.

What I join aren't fan clubs, but social groups. Book groups, women's groups, meditation groups — you name it, I've likely done it.

This has been a relatively recent development. Growing up, my mother was stubbornly independent, and I followed in her footsteps. Perhaps that's because the groups I saw then were either the too-traditional variety or ones that required funny hats to be a member.

But all that changed when I got my taste of THE group. When my kids were young, I started a book group in Phoenix. A friend of mine had moved to town and wanted to meet other women. So, I invited a few friends and asked them to all bring a friend. We met monthly in each others' homes, sharing a dessert, wine and the most illuminating, intimate conversation one could imagine. Once you walked through the door, you were completely yourself. Sometimes we dug so deeply we had profound insights about our own lives; other times, we laughed so hard we felt the stress of days or even weeks melt away. It was like a flash of that perfect Christmas — you experience it once and then try to recreate it forever more.

Not all groups have turned out this way. In some gatherings, people mix more like oil and water than a smooth wine hitting all the right notes. I've found myself nervously checking my watch, then fleeing with the screen door flapping behind me before final handshakes.

The ones that do work often have intimacy, curiosity and laughter; those that don't are where people enter with social masks on... and never take them off. It's like the sweater you want to love, but no matter how much you adjust, it still won't fit.

Just like there are friends for a reason or a season, so there are groups. An *Artist's Way* group I attended met at a hilltop house for 12 weeks — the exact number of chapters in the book. A more open-ended group met monthly and picked topics such as "What is Joy?" or "How Do I Handle Anger?" Each month, the leader would pick the subject, and for the next 30 days we'd all observe how that topic affected our lives. By the time we met, sitting in a circle with a candle flickering in the middle, we were primed for in-depth sharing. The best part was the buffet of different perspectives, each broadening and shedding light on my own.

Sometimes groups are created out of thin air, pulling together various friends to meet a certain need. I've had a writing focus group, and another looking at "what's next" in our lives.

One friend of mine spent hours sitting with the same handful of mothers watching their children at swim practice. Through casual conversation, they realized they all loved movies and a weekly movie group began. Another friend worked at hospice. After leaving, she called a few of her old hospice buddies and began a "Salon Sisters" group to discuss birth, death and everything in between.

One of my favorites was a small "yoga and brunch" group that met weekly. First we'd unroll our mats in the living room and practice downward-facing dogs and other poses for an hour. As we took deep, yogic breaths, we'd inhale the scent of bubbling soup or baking bread. Then, we'd head for the kitchen. Our Welsh hostess always had something homemade on hand, along with a warm pot of African Kwazulu tea. Hours would pass as we refilled dainty porcelain cups and talked about everything from doshas to diapers. This international community of women eventually morphed into a book group, which still meets today.

It's interesting how the groups we join reflect our aspirations of the moment. The yoga and brunch group fulfilled my need to tune into my body, as well as "nourish" myself through good food and close friendships. One woman I know joins local bunko and card groups to offset a feeling of alienation in her neighborhood. Exchanging information about pest control companies and recent births helps her feel connected. Yet another joins gourmet supper clubs to indulge her "Southern Living lifestyle" dream.

Although the types of groups out there grow more varied by the day, there's one thing they have in common. Everyone is there to connect, to find a friendly circle of faces in this increasingly fragmented society. We can do it alone. But, as any groupie knows, the show is so much more thrilling when shared.

Discover Your Own Pearls

Are you a groupie or a loner? Do you enjoy that balance? If you are in groups, are you sustained by all of them? Look at each one and see which ones energize you and which deplete you. Which add to your life? And if you've never been much of a joiner, try one out. Go a few times to really see the dynamics. Observe how you react. And most of all, enjoy!

OUR KIDS' FRIENDS

"Since there is nothing so well worth having as friends,
never lose a chance to make them."
— Francesco Guicciardini

I used to be annoyed by "those" parents. When there was an event that my kids and their friends wanted to attend, who wound up driving? Me. When they decided to have a party, whose house was it at? Ours. Or when the girls met a new friend, who broke the ice and extended an invitation? My children.

Why, I would grouse, are we always chauffeuring whereas Janie's parent (or Sally's or Jackie's...) never even offer to drive? Why do their kids intimately know the inside of our refrigerator, while my child has never even seen their front hall?

But, as usually happens when I get beyond my ranting and stop to think more deeply about it, I realized that my behavior is a choice. As is theirs. I stick to mine because it's based on a simple belief — getting to know your kids' friends is important.

When my daughter Chloe is hanging out with a friend at our house, I get to find out if her friend prefers challenging board games or mean-spirited gossiping. I get to see the interactions between Chloe and her friend, such as who is dominating the conversation, who isn't willing to compromise, who says "I'm bored" after two minutes verses who has endless ideas. Often I'm impressed by what I see. When I'm not, it's fodder for a good discussion with Chloe later that day.

I also get to see a different side of my child. My daughter Alix is relatively quiet around me, but I get to see a giggling, silly banshee around other kids. Since she's a teen, I'm always looking for more ways to connect with her. By getting to know her friends, my husband and I show that what's important to her is important to us. When she mentions a friend, the conversation is a lot more intimate when we respond with "Oh, Jill, you mean the one who..." rather than "Jill who?"

Our kids occasionally throw parties, which is a great way for them (and us) to get to know the more peripheral friends rather than just the core group. Other days, they call friends to join us on family outings that we were planning to do anyway — perhaps a hike or even just running errands. During the drive, we benefit from the fact that children think they're in an alternate universe in the car. They talk as if we don't exist. We "try" not to listen, although it never really works.

Parents are part of the package, too. I'm amazed at all the parents who have never met me, yet have no problem dropping their child at the curb and driving off... assuming, I imagine, that I won't be waiting at the door with a pit bull and a shotgun.

My husband and I always introduce ourselves to parents we don't know, taking an extra two minutes to shake hands and step inside their houses to get a feel for their lifestyle. Plus, you never know when getting to know them will come in handy. Last year, a boy Chloe had once been friends with decided to start harassing her. I hadn't seen his mother in years. Yet, because I had once made an effort to get to know her, I felt comfortable enough to call her. She talked to him and the problem ended.

Meeting the parents also points out red flags. Last spring, Chloe met a girl she liked in her acting class. I made a point of introducing myself to the girl's mother and started a casual conversation. That's when I found out that her oldest son was in jail for drug possession, but that the younger son's drug habit was improving daily!

Afterwards, in the car, I told Chloe that her friend seemed very nice. She could even come over sometime, but I didn't feel comfortable with Chloe going over to the girl's house to hang out.

To my surprise, Chloe looked deeply moved. She looked out the window for a moment, and then said with misty eyes that what I did meant a lot to her. It made her feel so loved, she added, that I had cared enough to find out about their family.

I suppose that's what it's all about, really. When we're involved with our children's friends, we're sending them a clear message. We care. Having their friends in our lives is a priority.

So, even though I may still complain now and again, deep down I know the truth. A few extra gallons of gas is a small price to pay for something you value — especially when it comes with miles worth of giggles.

Discover Your Own Pearls

How well do you know your children's acquaintances? Not just the core group, but the ones who sit with them on the bus or at lunch? The ones they hang out with in class? How often do you encourage your children to invite friends over? If the answer is not often, that's okay. Just be sure that's a choice you've consciously made, rather than a habit you've fallen into. Aim for the place where you feel good about the amount of time and connection you have with your children's friends.

TIPPING THE FRIENDSHIP SCALE

"Unlike dysfunction, healthy intimacy pulls away, bounces back, creates infinite fresh configurations. Trusting the rhythm of each relationship, rather than insisting on robotic consistency, will keep you from panicking when someone's boundaries move a bit toward or away from you."
— Martha Beck

There's math and there are friends. I'd never thought to put the two together until a few months ago when I came across an "intimacy scale." On it were descriptions of friends from 1-10, ranging from least to most intimate. "One," for instance, is the person you say hello to at a school event, but wouldn't want to spend a moment with otherwise. "Fives" are the scrapbooking or shopping buddies. "Tens" are the ones who you are truly yourself with. They come early to help you cook for a party and are the last to leave, opening the fridge and taking a finger scoop of cake icing on their way out.

For something as amorphous and complicated as friendship, I was intrigued that one could look at it from this more analytical perspective. According to Martha Beck, creator of this comrade calculator, most of our relationships ideally are in the middle of the scale, with a few people at either extreme. She says too many at the high end can lead to exhaustion and emotional overload; too many at the low end means you may be sending out "keep away" signals.

Perhaps that explains the emotional "glass ceiling" we

sometimes encounter. Have you ever had a friend you wanted to get to know better, only to get nowhere? They may be busy managing their numbers, keeping you in the range they have time or energy for. No matter how many times we meet them for lunch or spill our innermost feelings, nothing changes.

One woman I talked with said she had eight friends in the highest end of the scale and she sees all of them several times a week, socializing as their paths mingle at schools and neighborhood gatherings. She doesn't pursue closer relationships with "neighbor moms at the bus stops, school moms, scout parents and work-related relationships" because she simply doesn't have the energy.

More often, though, the women I talk with bemoan a lack of close friends. They have plenty at the bottom or middle of the scale, yet not enough soul-mates they can call at 2 a.m. in an emergency. They wonder if they risk enough emotionally with others and are vulnerable enough to form deeper friendships. Or if they have made time in their lives for others. When I recently looked at my pattern, I saw that while I was open in theory to closer friendships, I hadn't carved out time for them.

Mid-life women I chat with seem to feel that close relationships were easier to create when they were younger. One friend of mine in Phoenix says she had a lot of "10" friends before having kids. Or, as she says, the "pre-marriage, pre-parent, pre-mortgage, pre-PTO, pre-laundress and cook, me." Her local friends today are in the 2-5 range. With her old pals, she recalls fondly, she felt "less judged, funnier, more interesting…"

Of course, friends don't stay in a static place on the scale. When I've had major changes in my life, such as the death of my mother and the spiritual changes that accompanied it, all but the friends highest on my scale got shuffled around or even fell off completely. And when I reach new areas of growth, new friends seem to appear at these different levels.

Beck advises, "If thinking about one person makes you irritated or exhausted, you need to create more space in your dance with that person at that time. Decrease time and attention with them until you reach a level at which your irritation disappears. But if you want to be closer to some on the list, you'll feel curious and interested as you think about them. Ask them questions. If they open up, it will 'trigger a pleasant interchange of gradual, mutual self-disclosure.'"

While discovering the strengths and blind spots in my own patterns with friends has been an interesting adventure, ultimately it's not what matters. You can't weigh and measure where someone is on the scale because anyone is capable of being a "10" for a moment. Even a stranger.

That instant when you share a hearty laugh, or someone hugs you with compassion instead of judgment, is all that counts. In the end, a lifetime of those moments adds up to something immeasurable...

Discover Your Own Pearls

You saw this coming — yes, make a list of your friends and see where they fall on the scale. Then make a list of your friends from 20 years ago or childhood and see what the patterns were on the scale then. Finally, where would you ideally like friends to be on the scale today? Are there some people you need to move down the scale who you aren't connecting with as well as you'd like to? Some people who you'd like to open up with more to move them up the scale? Look at all the possibilities.

WORLD AROUND A BLOCK

*"... the more we love any that are not as we are,
the less we love as men and the more as God."*
— John Saltmarsh

The trick, I'd tell newcomers, is to always wear clean socks.

I was embarrassed many times before that simple fact sunk in. I'd arrive at an Indian acquaintance's house and be invited in for tea. Once through the threshold, though, I'd spot the telltale pile of shoes and freeze. Perhaps another time, I'd stammer. I knew full well that just below my shiny loafers were socks with stains so permanent no amount of Clorox could erase them.

Ah, the perils of foreign relations... in Texas.

When our family moved back to Austin a couple of years ago, I expected to find the laid-back, artsy little town I had left 15 years ago. What I found instead was a faster paced international community where I felt almost as if I was a foreigner in my own land. I'd have to learn a whole new set of "rules" as I tried to fit in with different cultures and make connections. It was a fascinating place to be, but it didn't feel like coming home.

One of the first clues that things had changed was a morning walk through our new neighborhood. When we used to live in Austin, I'd say "hi" to my yuppie neighbors or wave at the tattooed artist who sat sketching on her porch. Now, as I warmed my legs in the brisk air, an elderly Chinese man on a rickety bike slowly pedaled by me wearing a placid smile. Next I spotted an attractive woman in a bright yellow sari. As she got closer, I could hear the wail of a sitar streaming through her headphones. And two young men jogged by speaking a language I didn't even recognize, their pagers clipped securely to their running shorts.

As I finished my walk and returned home, I heard our neighbor's dog Mickey barking. I tried to shout "quiet," but to no avail. I later learned that "chup!" would have calmed him, since he only "speaks" Bengali.

I'm not sure how many languages the dogs in our neighborhood know, but at my daughter's elementary school, the children speak 25 different languages (not including the pig Latin voiced by mine). Making new friends took awhile because every time my daughters called to invite someone over, particularly the Asians, they were busy. While my girls were listening to music, others were learning to play violin and piano, pushing beads at abacus classes, kicking at karate, mastering Chinese, driving to Kumon and signing up for everything imaginable. While retrieving the morning paper on Fridays, we'd see more than 100 cars lined up at 6:45 — all dropping off their little soldiers for the school chess club.

Despite scheduling challenges, my daughters have pals regularly coming and going now. The hardest part — for me - has been remembering names. It was easy before — "Hi, Jane, how's it going?" Now, my middle school daughter has friends named Shivani, Sohini, Sanjoli, Sunanya and... Samantha. I felt like I'd earned a medal when they all came over for a party and I got all their names right. To complicate things even more, some have "pet" names and "real" names. Then again, there's Ruth. But don't let logic fool you — she's Chinese, not American.

For us, summers bring nearby trips to visit family in Missouri and New Mexico, while our friends jet set through faraway Europe and Asia, bringing back exotic tales and sometimes trinkets for the girls. Our next door neighbor, Roopa, graciously brought both of my daughters traditional ghaghras (skirts) from India.

They sometimes wear them around the house, but my daughter Alix has never worn it to Indian birthday parties. She'd feel out of place. Indian teens are wearing jeans and t-shirts. They order pizza, although an occasional curry is thrown in. They play games, watch movies, laugh, share stories. In other words, they do things all teens do, no matter what country they happen to be in.

When I go late at night to pick her up, I knock on the door and take my shoes off when I enter, dropping them into the colorful kaleidoscope of sandals, loafers and tennis shoes. She's reluctant to leave, and I often stay and chat, too. I admire these strong women, building a life someplace so far from what they know. They've become more to me than interesting conversationalists — they've become friends.

Finally, we retrieve our shoes and leave for home.

Home. Thinking about that word, I realize with a start that that's what Austin finally is for us again — home.

Discover Your Own Pearls

How many close friends are different from you, whether because of culture, income level, political leanings or something else? Is it the right mix for you? Note which qualities you embrace and which you'd rather change. Slowly dig a little deeper and see what's there.

OPEN-HEARTED LIVING

"It is only through letting our heart break that we discover something unexpected: the heart cannot actually break, it can only break open. When we feel both our love for this world and the pain of this world — together, at the same time — the heart breaks out of its shell. To live with an open heart is to experience life full-strength."
— John Welwood

I've been looking around Hallmark and haven't seen one yet. I've seen lots of condolence cards that say "Sorry for your loss" or "With great sympathy." Those are all noble sentiments. But I haven't yet found the ones I'm looking for, and something tells me I never will.

The cards I'm searching for would be tossed out of shops in two minutes. In our society, they wouldn't be understood. That's because they'd say something like, "We've heard of your broken heart — hope it never totally heals." Or "So you feel naked and vulnerable right now? Congratulations."

You might think I'm off my rocker, but frankly, those are the messages I wish I'd heard nine years ago when my mother died. Those are also the messages I tell myself today, three weeks after my father's death.

Many see grieving as a raw time that one should heal from as quickly as possible before getting back to "normal." But what if that business-as-usual lifestyle was really the one we needed to move beyond? What if we were meant live from that open, vulnerable heart rather than stitch it up and go back to efficient living and comfortable feelings?

Why would we want to do that? Why expose ourselves to pain? The irony here is that with openness we do feel pain… but we also feel pleasure. Deeply. When I'm brave enough to really feel my sadness, instead of boxing it up for another day, I also feel my wonder and joy. I step outside at dusk and watch the girls run up the street with the dog, yelping in their cold and excitement, and a profound, tender happiness thaws me.

Buddhist Chogyam Trungpa Rinpoche talks about being a warrior in life. Not a warrior in an aggressive sense, but in a courageous sense. He says, "Warriorship is so tender, without skin, without tissue, naked and raw. It is soft and gentle. You have renounced putting on a new suit of armor. You have renounced growing a thick, hard skin. You are willing to expose naked flesh, bone and marrow to the world."

I thought about that the other day. I was rushing to get dinner finished, and annoyed that Chloe hadn't yet finished her homework. I didn't stop to look at a school project my daughter Alix had done, said I'd get to it later. I dashed across the street to get the mail, oblivious to the cooler temperature and soft cumulus clouds floating over the treetops. I was a self-contained whirl of efficiency. When I finally stopped and realized that I was back to "normal" in that moment, living under the illusion that I didn't need to tune in and appreciate the moment — because of course there's always tomorrow — I was aghast. True, I felt no pain. I also felt no joy. My convenient armor was back in place.

I took that armor off as I remembered my father, a 6' 2", leonine man who spoke loudly and gave giant, gentle bear hugs. This week, his ashes will arrive in my mailbox. So when I see my daughters, I pull them towards me for a hug. I feel Chloe's heart beating underneath her fleece sweater, her fragile arms around me, the pulse of life and breath, and I say thank you, thank you. I watch the studious gaze of my older daughter and her pale hand lightly resting on a textbook, and I say thank you.

Instead of closing off my heart, I try to be as tender and vulnerable as a spring mushroom. I see my dad's old cap or a new moon or a baby's bottom, and my heart aches. I'm not used to the butterflies flitting against my skin. To the rawness. It's easy to charge into battle with that suit of armor on. You don't feel the arrows that might come your way, but you also don't see the spring daisies in the battlefield. Being naked is brave, difficult, satisfying and deeply worthwhile. It connects me to others. It's why we're here in the first place.

When I receive a card telling me that time will heal and soon life will be as before, I'll still send a quiet smile of appreciation to the sender. For how are they to know that I'd rather have a heart broken wide open than one all fixed up and sealed closed, tight as a coffin...

Discover Your Own Pearls

How deeply have you felt your life in the past days or weeks? Are you fully present or numbing out certain parts? Take a few quiet moments and ask yourself what you're afraid to feel. Trust that if you open up and feel, the pain will move on, leaving behind a gift of awareness...

Growing Pearls

As We Sow

"While we try to teach our children all about life,
our children teach us what life is all about."
— Angela Schwindt

As we drove to the vet's office, our 14-year-old yellow lab Cayce lying feebly in the back seat, I thought about how I'd comfort my daughters if we received bad news about her health. I'd have to be strong, dig deep to find reassuring words.

Thirty minutes later, standing in that sterile office with Cayce lying on the glistening silver table, he told us there wasn't much time left, perhaps a couple of weeks. Within seconds I was in tears, much to the surprise of the vet, while my dry-eyed daughters started scouring the room looking for tissues.

He left in polite embarrassment. What I remember most weren't his sad words, but the words of my daughter Alix. Eleven at the time, she looked up at me with great compassion, a calm presence, and uttered… the exact words I had planned to say to her.

She rubbed my back while talking about how Cayce had enjoyed a long life in a loving home. Alix continued that this was a painful moment, but that I should feel it fully and it would pass. That we needed to relish every last moment we had left with her and focus on life, not getting caught up in her impending death. And, did I need another tissue?

I didn't know what felt bigger at that moment, my sadness or my shock.

As a parent, you model, lecture and cajole, often believing that you're wasting your breath, that nothing's getting through to your kids. But then one day it happens. That thing you said when they were reading a book and didn't even glance at you comes out of their mouths. The lesson that you harped on without any visible change on their part suddenly becomes their mantra.

They come home from school having chosen loyal, hardworking friends whose clothes never match, and say — as if you're dense and need the lesson yourself — that it's what's on the inside that counts. Or they disappear into their rooms, once the nastiest place on the planet, and come out with half their belongings in boxes for Goodwill and say it was time to simplify.

We've all heard the words, "As you sow, so shall you reap." That's what parents do day after day. Sow, sow, sow. Pick up your wet towels, speak to your sister with respect, study hard, we robotically chant. The frustrating part is that we watch as absolutely nothing happens. We think we've failed. We don't understand how we can say the same thing twenty different ways with the same lack of result.

What we often forget is that miracles happen in their own time, not ours. Blooming isn't a command performance. The seed we throw out one day may take days or even years to blossom. Sometimes it won't at all. But all the while changes happen that are invisible to the eye.

Lately we've been watching this lesson play out on a smaller scale with our puppy. For weeks his favorite contraband was my soft maroon slippers. If they were unattended for even a moment, we'd see him pounce on one and take off with great glee. We kept sowing — no, release, no, release — and it seemed all we reaped were tattered slippers. But one day I spotted my slippers five inches from his nose, and instead of sneaking off with them he lay there, although his desire for them was obvious. He hasn't touched them since.

This doesn't just happen with our kids and pets. We plant seeds with our spouses, our friends, ourselves, yet grow impatient, even hopeless, when we think a change we so desire will never happen. We don't trust enough in the process. We're still pushing for our time, not the right time.

That day two years ago in the vet's office was the perfect moment for Alix's wisdom to appear. She had taken my words, then mixed them with her insights to create a message all her own. She still may not pick up her wet towels — that seed has yet to grow roots. But she touches many others with her compassion. That is why, as parents, we sow — so that the whole world may reap.

Discover Your Own Pearls

Think about some things you've been trying to change about yourself, whether it's a New Year's resolution to lose a few pounds or trying to take risks more often. These are the seeds you're sowing. Even if you're not seeing the results yet, have faith that change is happening that you can't see. Perhaps you're not losing weight, but you're learning more about healthy eating and a resolve is growing in a place you can't see yet. Keep planting and watch what grows next week, next year, and all the years to come...

VISITING NEVERLAND

"We have to listen to the child we once were, the child who still exists inside us. That child understands magic moments."
— Paolo Coelho

My daughter was only a few inches away from me, drifting off to sleep under her pink bedspread, and already I missed her. Just above our heads, the moon lit up a soft yellow spider's web made of yarn. She had spun it that day — her 9th birthday — and the breeze from the window shook it slightly. We had been to Peter Pan's Neverland, and I didn't want to go home...

Our first escape to Neverland was during lunch. Her aunt and grandparents came over and, after piling plates with food, we sat at the dining room table, as usual. We quietly chatted about small things, as usual. We were polite, as usual.

Then Chloe said she wanted to play "telephone" — that game we played as kids in which one person thinks of a sentence, then whispers it to the person next to them, and so on, until the last person says it aloud. My first instinct was to say no. After all, we were adults; there were certain unwritten rules on how adult lunches were conducted. But it was her birthday, so I relented. Before long, everyone at the table was foolishly giggling as the whispered messages got more garbled and silly with each person. We made faces. We crowed when our sentence was the funniest. We left our grown-up, responsible world and entered the web of childhood imagination. The rest of the day was a time to open our hearts, to take a leap to another place, a place we yearned for but didn't always know how to reach.

We hula-hooped. We lay on our backs and bounced the hover disc to one another with our feet. We animated thumb-sized dolls as they toured a tiny amusement park, spinning on saucers and flying from ride to ride. When we got hungry again, Chloe suggested breakfast for dinner. So, we all went to IHOP and feasted on pancakes and sausage, mixing different flavored syrups into runny messes on our plates.

As I relaxed in bed with her that night, I realized that even though we lived in the same house, it was far too rare that I completely entered her world, on her terms. I'm not talking about the daily interacting we do — clean your room, yes, you can go to Shelby's house, no, I'm too busy for Legos, have you eaten any fruit yet today? I'm talking about the times when you really stop everything — all that mental chatter, all your self-imposed deadlines — and become completely present and involved in a child's world.

The next day, I decided to carry some of the birthday magic into the rest of our lives. So, I asked Chloe if we could play with her Barbies. She looked at me with a rather patronizing look and said she was just heading out on her kick scooter, could we do it another time? I panicked. She was growing up, she didn't want to spend time with me anymore! So, I reached out to her on terms she could understand. Kid terms. I whined... Pleaaassee?

She relented, and we played Barbies, but I got very, very tired. So did she. That's when I realized I was doing it on my time again, with my control. But right then, with a child's intuitive sense, she came over and put her head on my tummy. Her body relaxed, and we just talked. Talked about what it would be like to be the last person on earth, about memories of our old dog Cayce. We went off to Neverland together.

I think my fear wasn't just that I'd miss out on deeply being a part of Chloe's childhood, but that somewhere along the way, I'd lost the child inside of me — the one who lay on the grass and stared at clouds, who belly-laughed for no good reason, who got so caught up in simple games that hours felt like minutes.

The other day we rented the movie Peter Pan, along with a projector. We hung a sheet on the wall to make it a "big screen" and covered the floor with pillows. As we snuggled amidst the pillows and ate tootsie pops, I felt like I was flying. Funny thing was, the movie hadn't even started…

Discover Your Own Pearls

Try a day — or even 30 minutes — of letting your child be in charge. Let them select the activities and the snacks. Go into it with an open, playful mind. If you don't have children, try it with a niece, nephew or a neighbor's child. Open your heart and see through their eyes for a while.

FULL SPEED AHEAD

*"Too many people grow up. That's the real trouble with the world,
too many people grow up. They forget.
They don't remember what it's like to be 12 years old.
They patronize, they treat children as inferiors."*
— Walt Disney

You'd think I'd have seen it coming. Picked up on the clues. Like the fact that my daughter Alix isn't in diapers anymore. Already knows how to ride a bike. Ok, and there's that catalog by her bed, too. The one listing courses for high school — she starts next year.

But no. I have that parental blind spot, like the one in my car's side mirror. Just when I think I know all the upcoming obstacles, one suddenly appears out of nowhere and I have to adjust. Quickly.

I had been cruising along, treating her as I always had — namely, in that slightly smothering, you are my child and I know best way. In my complacency, I didn't hear her adolescent rumblings until the evening the collision came.

It wasn't anything earth shattering, at least outwardly. It was a school night and time for bed. I said time for bed; she said she wanted to stay up. I repeated myself, so did she.

In the past, the unspoken agreement was that bedtimes were decided by me, carried out by her. No discussion. But this time was different. Suddenly I watched as she swelled up to her full power — like a peacock who has kept his feathers hidden and then suddenly fluffs up to become an imposing presence — and then she uttered these words, "You know, mom, you can't make me go to bed if I don't want to."

I know, some of you are saying no big deal. My kid says that all the time. But our pattern had been different. We had our roadblocks and U-turns, but defiance wasn't one of them. This was a fork in the road, a road we'd never been down before. I just stood there, mute and enraged, and then strode off to figure out what to do.

My first thought was to bark a Gestapo-like threat for her to march upstairs or face dire consequences. But in my heart I knew that wasn't the solution. I resisted the temptation to give her the silent treatment — the ammunition of my own teenage years.

Short of answers, I descended on our bookshelves, pulling out volume after volume, but only coming up with titles like "Winning the War against Whining" and "The Growing Years," which in the author's opinion ended at age 12. Alix was almost 14. I finally got on Google, but "what to do when your teenager grows up and you hadn't noticed and now haven't a clue as to the next step" wasn't in there.

I went upstairs and wandered into my 9-year-old daughter's room. She slept under her bed canopy like a fairytale princess, blonde locks framing her face, her tiny body curled around a pillow. This I knew. This age in parenting I had gotten down — at least occasionally. This was where I wanted to freeze time.

Finally, I wandered into my teen's room, where she was now in bed reading. As I walked in, I noticed her clothes responsibly laid out for school the next day. I thought of how compassionately she had comforted her sister the day before, and how when she stood to give me a hug, I was looking into the eyes of a beautiful woman exactly the same height as I. She was growing up.

That's when I realized that I don't want a fairytale teen who is always meek and lovely. My husband and I have done our job of raising a daughter who thinks for herself and expresses it, whether raging over injustices in other countries or writing fervent poems. Every now and again that passion spills out in unforeseen directions, but that's okay.

That evening we sat and talked. Ends up, her outburst was fatigue and built up frustration from not being given more choices in her life. My husband and I were still steering the car, even on those gentle roads that she could navigate herself. We needed more discussion, less dictating. It was agreed that bedtimes were one area we could tweak... with her input.

I've now tossed the parenting books because it's clear she's no longer a little girl. Instead, Alix and I are creating the maps as we go. Sometimes we veer off the road in a flash of anger, other times our relationship is a joyride on a Sunday afternoon. Either way, I pay attention, for every mile of the journey is worth savoring.

Discover Your Own Pearls

Are you staying in tune with your children as they're growing? It's hard to see change when you're living with them every day, but think back to how they were a year ago. Two years. Is there an area where they've changed and perhaps you need to adjust? Bottom line — listen more, talk less. That's something they need at any age.

SHIFTING GEARS

"We do not grow absolutely, chronologically. We grow sometimes in one dimension, and not in another; unevenly. We grow partially. We are relative. We are mature in one realm, childish in another. The past, present, and future mingle and pull us backward, forward, or fix us in the present. We are made up of layers, cells, constellations."
— Anais Nin

We tried to resuscitate her. It had always worked before, but this time she finally gave her death rattle — a noisy flurry of car doors locking and unlocking while something ticked under the hood. Finally, she rested by the curb and became quiet. My old green mini-van was a goner… along with a chunk of my mothering identity.

We had gotten her years ago, back when Chloe was just three and Alix seven. They dubbed her "Mama Green." Back then, what I wanted was clear cut. Lots of drink holders for sippy cups, fabric that would hide the stains, something big enough to hold car seats, balls, friends, diaper bags and a large dog. The key word was practical.

The years took their toll — a stain here, a dent there. The new car gleam faded as she opened her doors to all of life, from muddy hiking boots to gymnastics over the seats when I wasn't looking. After a while, she became invisible.

But then vehicular Alzheimer's set in. Some days she remembered how to start, other days she didn't. I would jump in with Alix, slinging the school backpack in the back seat while hurriedly switching on the ignition, only to hear the choked thwack of a dying motor. On those mornings, I'd sprint down our still darkened street looking for a neighbor to drive her to school.

But even that didn't convince me to sell her.

I could relate to her. My youth was going, too. I had gone from jet-set travel writer to practical mom, totally giving myself over to the job. My wardrobe through the years had grown more practical, less stylish. My hair was always brushed... but not much more. Makeup was an optional luxury for when I had extra time. My sheen had worn off, too. I was all about the inside, not the packaging.

When Mama Green finally conked out, I headed to the car lots looking for something new. But the decision wasn't as easy as it was when I bought her. Part of me wanted the comfort of the past, a big 'ol "stuff" machine with lots of seats and pockets and space. But another part was remembering the pre-kids Carolyn with her shiny red Toyota Celica jazzed up with spoilers. That part wanted something fun, stylish. Perhaps a bit impractical? A bit of high heel verses worn down sneaker?

Without knowing it, I was really trying to figure out who I was. My girls are 10 and 14 — one in high school and one starting middle school next year. I'm not a mother of toddlers, motherhood with a capital "M" stamped on my forehead. But I still have a few years before they're both out of the house. I'm in the middle and moving closer to the day when my identity will shift in other directions.

Last week we finally bought a new vehicle — a shiny gold Nissan Murano with sunroof, Bose stereo and five especially luxurious leather seats. I thought I had reached nirvana. Gone was the matronly swing of the mini-van. In its place was a cute rear end that I didn't even have to diet to achieve.

This is bliss, I thought as I turned the corner by Alix's school one day. Suddenly, though, it hit me that her prom was coming up and all her friends wouldn't fit into this smaller car. That's when I lost it.

I hadn't realized just how much my vehicle was an

extension of me. By losing two extra seats, I felt like part of my mothering ability was cut off. How could I hold all the love and mothering I had left without the spacious arms of a bigger vehicle? What if they needed something and, God forbid, I couldn't provide it? What if our lives shrunk to fit the size of the car?

For several days, I was in a panic about having made the wrong choice. I couldn't see anything but two missing seats. But slowly I got seduced by the view of the moon through the sunroof, by the seats that heated my worn body when I climbed in on brisk mornings. I melted into having a vehicle that pampered me, rather than me always pampering others.

I still have moments when I miss that third row of seats, when I miss the past. But there are also times when I'm enjoying this newfound luxury and reaching out tentatively towards my own freedom. Gears are shifting... and not just the ones in my car.

Discover Your Own Pearls

Where are you in your journey as a mother, a daughter, a friend or a spouse? What are you ready to leave in the past... and what wonderful things do you imagine for yourself in the future? Perhaps you can let something go in order to grab hold of what's next?

SCHOOL'S IN... MOM'S OUT

"To "let go" does not mean to stop caring, it means "I can't do it for someone else." To "let go" is not to enable, but to allow learning from natural consequences. To "let go" is not to care for, but to care about. To "let go" is not to fix, but to be supportive. To "let go" is not to be in the middle arranging all the outcomes, but to allow others to effect their destinies. To "let go" is not to be protective, it's to permit another to face reality."
— Unknown

Now I know why high schools were invented. Contrary to popular belief, it's not just to further our children's education. Oh no, there's a much sneakier plan at work here. It's to keep out mothers like me. Mothers who, were it not for those locked doors and chilling teenage stares, would still be arriving at school with cupcakes and an extra sweater. It's for those of us who believe "letting go" is a term used for extra weight and stray animals — not our children.

When my oldest daughter, Alix, started high school, I thought I'd inconspicuously mosey on in with her. Problem is, the administrators know my type. While there are over a hundred parking spaces at the school, fewer than a dozen are marked for visitors. And I imagine the other freshmen moms beat me to it, because all were filled when we arrived on the first day.

My fantasy had been to go in with her, a map-reading

sidekick who would help her through the labyrinth of beige hallways. Perhaps I'd say a friendly "hello" to her first teacher, surreptitiously handing him a three-page synopsis of some of her better qualities. Might come in handy — especially when a hundred other nameless students stream through.

I could even pop by the school nurse with a bottle of lavender oil on hand, explaining that a few drops on Alix's temples help when she gets a headache. Looking around, I might even point out that a few more cheery pictures would do, along with some snuggly afghans, before I headed out to stick a couple of smiley faces on my daughter's locker.

However, unable to park that morning, I reluctantly slithered in the line of cars towards the drop-off area. Do you have your tissues, I queried? A few pens? What about your schedule? Relieved, I imagine, to be free of me — yet just as reluctant to leave the car — she gathered her things and flashed a "I hope I survive this" smile before disappearing into the blur of backpacks and lanky students.

I kept waving and watching, even after she was gone, but the line of cars gently urged me not to loiter, that it was time to move on…

It seemed easier in elementary school. Rather than keeping us out, these schools begged parents to get involved. Hallways bright with messy paintings embraced us. We read stories to adoring pupils, joined them for chicken nuggets and Jell-o in the cafeteria, and returned from field trips with hay in our shoes. We felt needed; they felt loved.

These cold metal doors that clang shut behind our high school students are a whole other matter.

The first week of school, Alix came home with stories. I heard how freshmen, or "fish" as they're called, have to jockey for seats in the cafeteria. One has to figure out which seats are unofficially "taken," so as not to accidentally sit in a senior's favorite spot and suffer the consequences. Groups of friends shifted, with some deciding they were too "cool" to be sociable anymore.

Rules tightened. Just a handful of absences affect your grades. Pneumonia isn't an excuse. Neither is a mother coming in saying things didn't seem quite fair, could they kindly make a few changes? And add cushions on those horrible plastic chairs while they're at it?

As I stewed, I decided to walk off my frustration with a friend. She'd been there. Some of her boys were already off to college. As we rounded the scenic hills of the neighborhood, a school bus roared by belching gray smoke, student faces staring out the windows. You know, she said after listening to me, mothers often forget that you raise your children to prepare them to leave the nest. To survive on their own.

I blinked. I bumbled. And then I got it.

That's why high schools keep us out. Because if they didn't, our protective mothering instinct would go into overdrive trying to fix all the new challenges for them. The cliques. The competition. The tough assignments. All the rough edges that we've spent our lives softening.

Yet by stepping back, we give our children room to step forward. We give them enough space to stumble, feel their pain, and then get up again with renewed strength and wisdom. I realize that I am no longer meant to be the conquering heroine clearing a path for the delicate maiden. I am meant to be a safe harbor where she can return after a day of slaying dragons, for she'll soon discover she's powerful enough to face them on her own.

Discover Your Own Pearls

What is your relationship to your child's school life? Are you there at every corner, or do you not even know the name of his or her teacher? Whose needs are being met by your involvement or lack thereof — yours or theirs? Is it the right balance for both of you? If you're not sure of these answers, sit down and talk with your child about where ideally he or she would like more of your help... and where less is more.

GERM WARFARE

"Let us rise up and be thankful, for if we didn't learn a lot today,
at least we learned a little, and if we didn't learn a little,
at least we didn't get sick, and if we got sick,
at least we didn't die; so, let us all be thankful."
— Buddha

They came undercover. That's how the sneaky devils work. My daughter Chloe came home from school and showed me a trail of bug bites on her back. When I looked further, I saw that the dang bugs had walked all the way across her body, a marathon feeding feast with a bit of neck here, some shoulder blade there.

Perplexed, I called my husband Charley and described the bites. He let out that patient sigh I've heard so many times before, then answered, "Have you thought of chicken pox?"

Of course I hadn't. She'd been vaccinated, I said. But after a quick look online, I realized a simple shot is no guarantee. She'd caught it anyway.

All this would have been bad enough, but in addition I knew I could come down with it since I'd never had it before. Plus, my oldest daughter goes to a high school notorious for its rigorous academics and overextended students. If she got it, catching up on schoolwork afterwards would mean she'd emerge from her studies just long enough to eat and hand me her laundry. "Luxuries" like showers and sleep would go by the wayside.

So, she did what any caring, compassionate sister would do. She treated Chloe like a leper. In a nice way, of course. The germ warfare had begun.

First, the kitchen towels were separated. Chloe had her "poxy" towel hanging in one place, Alix and the rest of us used another. We fought with chemical warfare, spraying canisters of Lysol in hopes of hitting an enemy we couldn't even see. Everything Alix, my husband and I touched provoked anxiety. Had Chloe touched it? What was the likelihood she'd picked up this section of the newspaper, or had twisted open the back door handle? When we saw a sneeze coming, we'd scramble for cover.

It got even worse for all of us when a secondary infection kicked in and Chloe was up half the night coughing. We slumped in steamy bathrooms at 3 a.m. as the moisture melted hair, clothes and coughs.

The next day I called my friend Barb, a nurse training to be a naturopath, and asked what we could do to buck up our immune systems. She gave me a list and sent me to a funky little health food store promoting the benefits of bee pollen and essential oils.

After I got home, we started pouring potions, popping pills and massaging creams. Alix spent most of her time quarantined in her room. Chloe hugged the dog, the only one who unabashedly snuggled with her. I'd give her a quick hug, then imagine I could see the germs clinging to my clothes, shaking a fist and saying "We'll get you yet!"

Finally, we decided to take Alix to her grandparents' house to give her a break.

The next morning, her grandmother called. Well, she said in her sweet Texas drawl, looks like my husband is coming down with something. Better pick her up.

That's when it hit me. Not the chicken pox, but the realization that we'd spent nearly a month-long siege running from something we couldn't hide from anyway. The more energy I spent worrying about if she had sipped from this water glass or coughed onto that remote control, the less energy I had to keep my own body strong. Mentally, I'd been getting drained instead of filling up. It was time for a massage, a relaxing book and a hefty dose of surrender. I felt better immediately.

As it ended up, Alix didn't get chicken pox. At least she hasn't yet. Evidently it can take as long as 21 days to show up. But I figure why worry about what you can't control? Meantime, I'll relax and enjoy life... along with a few extra vitamin C tablets.

Discover Your Own Pearls

When someone in your family gets sick, how much time do you spend worrying about it? How much control do you have over that situation? What different thought patterns might be more effective for you? If nothing else, have a good laugh — it'll make everyone feel better!

KIDS' HIGH-TECH RITES OF PASSAGE

*"People are very open-minded about new things —
as long as they're exactly like the old ones.*
— Charles Kettering

When our daughters were babies, I always imagined what it would be like when they got their "firsts." First bicycle, first prom, first car. I'd chortle knowingly about their combination of anxiety and excitement. Then I'd start in on the stories. Oh, I know just how you feel, I'd say with nostalgia. I remember back when I got my first bicycle. It was cherry red and the spring leaves were just beginning to bud...

Next would come the advice. Now remember, these gears can be tricky. The easiest thing is to start in 3rd gear, then adjust slowly, I'd say.

Well, last week we hit a first with our daughter Chloe. She'd been wanting a cell phone for more than a year, but we didn't see a need for it. This year, she started middle school and we found ourselves wishing for a phone as she expanded into extracurricular activities and new friendships.

Before long, a shiny, silver flip phone arrived at the house. As she pulled off the cellophane of this pocket-sized "first," I realized I had no similar childhood memory to dredge up. When I was her age, we were still using rotary dial on the bulky phone anchored to the kitchen counter, its 6-foot cord hopelessly twisted from all the pacing we did while talking.

So, I decided to move right on to the sage instructions. You have a phone now, I said knowingly as I held it in my hand. Suddenly the words "activate PTT" popped up on the tiny phone screen, and I concluded my profound advice with "How the heck do you use it?"

I had no advice at all. A first had come — for me.

The next day, not to be bested, I got out the phone's instructions. I sat down in the old lazy-boy chair — similar to the one in our den as I grew up — and opened the "Quick Start" guide as I drank my tea. It said she could print photos wirelessly to a Bluetooth printer, whatever that was. With some "PTT" thing, she could instantly speak with up to 30 people. That might come in handy when planning another rite of passage — her wedding — but I couldn't understand its use now. Not only could she take pictures, but it also advised one could "share them instantly with friends via multimedia messaging." Plus, it offered ring tones from today's "hottest performers." This was all in the 6-page start-up guide; I had yet to crack open the 107-page main manual.

Then I saw the health alerts. It said that by using the phone, users may be susceptible to potentially hazardous Electro Magnetic Field Emissions (EMF) radiation. Children, I found out as I frantically searched online for more information, are at the most risk.

By the time she got home from her friend's house, riding her scooter down our tranquil suburban street with cell phone happily tucked in her pocket, I was on the verge of grabbing this confusing, dangerous little gadget and stomping on it.

I had the same feeling I did when I let her have her own e-mail. I was excited for her, but also fearful because of all I didn't know. There was no wisdom of hard won lessons to share with her, nothing I could offer to protect her from perils even I couldn't imagine. Inappropriate spam. Cyber bullying. Predators.

With a flip of a phone and click of a mouse, things have changed. In this turbulent high-tech arena, I'm no longer the fearless leader. I'm the fellow pioneer, trying to avoid land mines as I explore with my daughters' this uncharted territory, both thrilling and dangerous. This equal footing feels new. In fact, for us, it's a first.

Discover Your Own Pearls

What are some of the "firsts" you've shared with your children, nieces or nephews? When do you feel like the one giving advice? When are you "getting advice?" How does the switch feel for you? When new technology becomes available for your kids, do you freeze up and turn the other way or leap and buy without careful consideration? Are you happy with that balance?

EASILY AMUSED

"When people are laughing,
they're generally not killing one another."
— Alan Alda

Sometimes I'm easily amused. Like right now. As I write these words, I think that a moose (or a cow) would be easily amoosed. An emu would be easily emused. And you're probably easily confused.

But that's beside the point. Or is it? Last week, when my middle school daughter came home from her UIL band contest, she made the observation that kids her age were "easily amused." It was, she said, her new mantra. In fact, she wanted it on a t-shirt.

That got me thinking. We strive to be many things — thin, peaceful, organized, wealthy — but not, it seems, easily amused. Maybe that's because these words carry baggage. Often, they come right after the word "not," as in, "I'm not easily amused!" — something that the substitute teacher might shriek after finding a frog in her chair in one of those 1950's sitcoms.

Yet, when I started playing with those two words, I found they had so much more to offer. They inspire a certain lightheartedness, a playfulness. If I walk out the door in an "easily amused" state of mind, I'm ready to be surprised and delighted by anything, from a squirrel rocketing off a branch after threats from an angry bluebird, to a garbage collector wearing high heels.

Or, I can create my own amusement, like the kids on Alix's band bus did. They left miles of giggles along the highway as they caught the road-glazed eyes of truck drivers and signaled for them to honk. One toot and they were in hysterics.

Later that day, while waiting an hour for a late bus to pick them up, they didn't get on cell phones and chew someone out. They didn't calculate taxes in their head or worry if there were enough crafts for the Girl Scout meeting. They didn't wallow, complain or vent. Instead, those pre-teens went straight to easily amused. They tossed their shoes to see how high they'd bounce. What was the trajectory? Would they go left, or right? Then they pointed at passing planes, "balancing" them on the tips of their fingers.

They created amusement by being open to possibility. By giving their imaginations some space to float, they could playfully paw their whims like a cat with a string.

Sometimes, of course, life can seem anything but amusing. And that, as we all know, is when we most need a good dose of merriment, an absurdity to slap us from our death grip on worry. That's how I felt one day while attempting to get Alix to her dance class, simmering in my own frustrations as I hit every red light, a funeral procession and finally a car accident that had shut down the road entirely, leading us on a mazelike detour through the neighborhood. After finally dropping her off, I stopped by Jack in the Box to placate my mood with monster tacos. The line of cars outside was daunting, so I parked and ordered inside. And waited. And waited. As my frustration morphed into anger, a gentleman walked up to me and apologized. He said it was probably his fault that the wait was so long. He had, after all, ordered 45 hamburgers.

Forty-five hamburgers! What next! The absurdity was just too much and I burst out laughing, perhaps even a tad uncontrollably, but that blasted me right from frustration to mirth and happily dropped me into "easily amused" for the rest of the afternoon.

"A good laugh helps us recognize how ridiculous it is to get excited about matters that are often trivial," says Arthur Asa Berger. Sometimes we get so caught up in our everyday struggles that we forget to step back and see the comedy of it.

One day I did homework with my daughter Chloe... shouting through a closed window. She was mad at me, so she chose to communicate from outside, yelping every so often as she accidentally brushed the prickly bush under the window. As my anger grew, suddenly I remembered I had another choice. I could instead see the wonderful silliness of the situation. In an instant, my irritation changed into amusement. And once I could laugh at the situation, so could Chloe.

The next day, I went with Alix to buy a t-shirt with her new mantra on it. We told the fellow at the counter what we wanted. He laid down the letters and, before pressing them on, asked us to check them. We looked. There in big red letters, no kidding, were the words "Easily Amussed."

Alix and I looked at each other with a sly chuckle. When we pointed out the spelling mistake, he was very apologetic. But he needn't have been... we're easily amused.

Discover Your Own Pearls

Where in your life do you tend to get overly serious? Paying taxes? Driving in rush hour? How can you transform that moment into something more amusing? As a reminder to lighten up, write the words "Easily Amused" in wacky, pink lipstick letters on your bathroom mirror...

BACK IN THE BEAT

*"The success of a creative recovery hinges on our ability to move out
of the head and into action. This brings us squarely to risk. Most of
us are practiced at talking ourselves out of risk. We are skilled
speculators on the probable pain of self-exposure."*
— Julia Cameron

It was bigger than I, that cello I had in sixth grade. Yet
every day I lugged it to school and back, awaiting that one
moment. Kids I had passed in the halls would gather
together in the old music room, our math books and grudges
left behind, and we would play. The very vibration lifted me. I
was smack in the middle of the music, sliding off the notes
and clanging with the cymbals.

Eventually, though, I left the cello behind. Years went by,
and while I almost unconsciously swayed when I heard music,
I didn't pick up any instruments myself. In fact, at some point
I started believing I couldn't play anymore. It wasn't my gift.
Leave the music making to people with real talent, I told
myself. Don't embarrass yourself.

Fast forward to my mid-twenties. I'm in the Ozark
mountains working on a story when someone asks me if I'd
like to go to a "shindig" at their home that evening. Sure, I say.
I arrive late, and can hear the music as I'm walking towards
the lights of the house, frost glittering from the windowpanes.
The door opens and the music sashays out to meet me, gives
me a spin and draws me into the living room. There, people

are playing fiddles and dulcimers, passing around fried pies, laughing. This is how we entertain ourselves on Saturday nights, the host explains. As the evening wears on, tired babies are wrapped in shawls and laid on the pile of coats to sleep. The fire crackles as the dulcimer sings its story. Voices rise and fall. I leave wishing I lived in the mountains, surrounded by music.

One day my husband comes home from a trip to California with a five-foot long, narrow package. He unwraps a wooden didgeridoo. The aborigines play these, he explains. He toots into it and the dog barks, jumps back. Soon he's playing daily, setting aside his stuffy business suit to meet a dreadlocked instructor on the shores of Barton Springs, learning how to keep time with the wings of birds, the slap of water.

I circle it, fascinated. Yet something stops me from picking it up. It's that same voice that talks to people who want to write, or dance, or sketch the daisies in their back yard. You enjoyed it as a child, it says. You won't have time to practice. You'll never get good enough to do it, let alone share it with others.

A short time later, my sister's friend Brad calls from St. Louis. He's a Native American flute player. Can he stop in and visit, he asks? Sure, I say, dusting off the tables and hiding the clutter. He arrives like the pied piper, flute in hand, and begins to play, calling moonlit nights and howling coyotes into our den. The very air changes. Not to be left out, my 10-year-old daughter Chloe grabs a souvenir drum we bought on vacation. She enthusiastically beats on it. My husband starts blowing into his didgeridoo; my oldest daughter Alix dances.

Then Brad opens his case and pulls out another flute, handing it to me.

Try, he says.

Pablo Picasso once said, "Every child is an artist. The problem is how to remain an artist once he grows up." I realize there's a girl with a cello, waiting.

So I pick up the flute. A sound comes out, one rusty squeak. A lisping whine. Brad gives me a few tips. I try again, and another note comes out, getting stronger, sailing through the den to greet the drum before it falls flat. I try again and suddenly something approximating a beat begins filling up the room.

Like toddlers left in the kitchen with the pots and pans, we begin to clang and exchange instruments, reveling in the unlikely, imperfect fun of it all. A stick ka-chings along the back of a chair; a spatula taps on the table. Alix glides through the room. I'm back in that 6th grade music room, in the middle of the music, hypnotized by beat and breath.

Soon I'm "jamming" with friends and family, and before long I have my own flute, hand-carved for me by my husband. We pass around the chips, laugh at our sometimes ridiculous music, and play. Everyone has a good time... especially the little girl with the cello.

Discover Your Own Pearls

What were some of the hobbies and activities you enjoyed as a child? Did you pursue them? If not, why? If this interest still whispers to you, how can you open your life to accommodate it? Feel the direction your heart wants to go, then take one small step towards making it happen.

SUMMER

"In the depth of winter, I finally learned that within me
there lay an invincible summer."
— Albert Camus

I could listen to the whir of the rattling air conditioner for hours it seems, so thick is the heat, so languid the day. Even the bugs scuttling by me on the porch go slowly, fat waddles, resting every few steps. Scooters lay on their sides, abandoned for other play, other dreams.

Every season has its pace, and for summer we're not talking the cha-cha. It's slow dancing, the far off cries of children seemingly lost in time. Is it today, or is it really summer of 1972 and I'm walking on stilts in my back yard, or building rickety forts in the empty lot across the street?

Summer offers freedom and possibility, but not immediately, especially for kids newly released from the discipline and routine of school. At first, my newly teenaged daughter Alix slept. A lot. My 9-year-old daughter Chloe had grown so used to following orders she forgot how to follow her own, how to entertain herself through long days without structure. But before long, I'd find Chloe lying under her ceiling fan creating fantasy worlds with tinker toys. Alix sat cross-legged under a tree writing poetry. Days began when the sun grew intense enough to wake them and wound down with the drone of cicadas in the trees.

Not everyone was like that. Some families scheduled their children from alarm ring to lights out, choosing the equivalent of summer home schooling. Summer was a time to catch up in weaker subjects or to one-up the competition in stronger subjects. Math facts cut through the stillness of late afternoon, constant chauffeuring shattered the day. Was I a deficient parent, I wondered? Perhaps I went too far the other way? I saw summer as this big blank canvas and watched them create their worlds, like in the book "Harold and the Purple Crayon." And as they formed their worlds, they got a chance to re-form themselves. As they slowed, joy came.

So summer went by. We caught fireflies. We waded through the shallow waters of Bull Creek. We lay on cool, white leather couches with a good book and dirty feet from running in the grass. Minds drifted with the clouds.

One day, Alix began daydreaming a party. An end of summer party. She contacted two of her close friends and they started planning. The more they had emptied out during the summer, the more space their imaginations had to roam. They spent afternoons giggling and imagining. Wasps buzzed outside the windows where they talked. Summer rains came and went. The party, they decided — knowing no bounds as summer had taught them — wouldn't be in the evening but would last from breakfast to dinner. A "ship" began to arise in our backyard. At another house, they lay on their stomachs and created a 21-foot dragon to wrap around the staircase, breathing red paper fire off the balcony. Underwater worlds of fish with mohawks swam in crepe paper waves.

The day of the party, a dozen 13-year-old girls came together simply to play. Being "cool" didn't matter. They reveled in their boundless summer, shrieking in wading pools, twirling on a disc hung from an oak tree. Inhibitions melted and friendships bloomed.

Now summer is coming to a close, or at least the school district's version of it. My younger daughter went to her school yesterday and pushed through the crowded cafeteria punctuated with ringing cell phones to find her name on the list. Then, students were marched to classrooms to organize their supplies, red construction paper in this pile, green in that, pencils here, blue books there.

Somewhat frazzled and sped up, afterwards we walked home. But as I looked around, the trees still hula danced slowly in the breeze. A fat lizard stared and blinked from the fence. Summer was still cajoling us to slow down, to appreciate, to learn its lesson for more than just a season...

Discover Your Own Pearls

When you look back at this past summer, what memories come up? What do you regret that you didn't do? What happy memories do you have of childhood summers that you could recreate, such as swinging or walking barefoot through the grass? And finally, what did you learn from the summer (slowing down, having trips for ice-cream with one child at a time) that you can use all year long?

Moment-to-Moment Pearls

CREATIVE PLAY

"To live a creative life, we must lose our fear of being wrong."
— Joseph Chilton Pearce

I was just drying my last saucer when I heard the crash in the driveway. Dropping the towel, I ran outside. There I found my husband Charley balancing atop a ladder holding one of his coveted clay sculptures. Before I could get a word out — crash! — it dropped on the driveway and shattered in an explosion of blue and gray. My daughters cheered, then handed him another pot. Rock music blared. On this beautiful, cloudless afternoon, while the neighbors mowed their lawns and the birds sang, my husband demolished his work — with a huge smile on his face.

It all started several years ago when Charley picked up ceramic sculpting as a hobby. He'd spend every Saturday morning at a studio having coffee and tacos with other artists and working clay into irreverent shapes. It was a welcome diversion from his hectic workday job, a stress-busting, bliss-inducing few hours every week. Later the studio moved into our garage, the pieces became more sophisticated, his plans for them more grandiose. Some even sold.

Odd thing, though. The better he got, the less he enjoyed it. Charley would go in his studio with big aspirations, and return a while later defeated and frustrated. He had one idea, the clay had another.

I knew the feeling well. Sometimes when I sit down to write, the words flow like honey and my tensions melt away.

But other times, especially when an important deadline is approaching, it can feel less like a frolic on the beach and more like trudging through quicksand. Sentences whip their heads around like 200-pound alligators ready to attack. The more I push myself to write — and make it good — the less I can eke out.

That's when I just need to back off and do my "bad writing." Play on the page and let the nonsense and bad metaphors muddy up the white space. Focus on movement, not miracles.

That day, as Charley gleefully demolished all but his favorite pieces, he got it. It's not about product, it's about process. It's not about how many wonderful sculptures one can create, each more perfect than the other and destined to land on the shelves of galleries to an adoring public. It's about the process of making them.

When he goes in his studio with the mindset of a child playing in the mud, poking in sticks for flagpoles and berries for color, it becomes play. No preconceived notions. No baggage from yesterday. Just playing in the moment, experimenting, taking risks. "Smashing" what came before, open to what comes next. That's when the passion returns.

As creativity coach Julie Cameron says, "'I am writing a screenplay' is infinitely more interesting to the soul than 'I have written a screenplay,' which pleases the ego. When focused on process, our creative life retains a sense of adventure."

When I write with this playful attitude, I can toss words around like hacky sacks to see where they land. I watch them flip and fly. But when I start getting stiff and serious about my writing, I find I'm that way about my life, too. Nothing sings. I cook dinner to get it finished quickly, rather than slowly swirling the spaghetti sauce with a wooden spatula, inhaling the pungent parmesan as I grate it by hand. Plates are flung on the table like haphazard Frisbees, not mindfully placed with order and pleasure. I drive to the library, thinking about the overdue fines I'll pay upon arrival, oblivious to the newly opened bluebonnets along the road.

Or I find myself in conversations like the one with my daughter Chloe's acting teacher. I was commenting on the fact that Chloe had only four lines in the upcoming play. In my mind, such talent deserved a much bigger role. In an instant, my ego had taken over. I had forgotten that the reason she was taking the class wasn't for five minutes of fame on stage, but the hours of play, improvisation, learning and fun that preceded it.

That doesn't mean the process toward a goal is non-stop fun. It's not. But there's a difference between a child playing and then tripping, feeling the pain, and moving on, and someone who won't take that first step. Or someone whose only pace is a serious, studied walk towards an "important" goal. The journey flies by unnoticed, never to return.

The other day I heard an earthy, melodic noise coming from the garage. I wandered out there and found Charley making clay whistles, blowing air through one that looked like a lopsided squash. He grinned at me like an impish 8-year-old. He picked up another misshapen lump of clay and gleefully blew. It was the sweetest sound I'd heard in a long time...

Discover Your Own Pearls

What are your creative activities — cooking, painting, singing in the shower? Have they lost their appeal or are they still appealing to you? If they're not as inspiring or interesting as they used to be, try listening to what you're telling yourself as you're doing them. Is it "I have to hurry up and do this because more important work is waiting" or "It's not good enough" or "I'm too old/busy/inept to start this?" Instead, just start. Let yourself do it badly, just for fun.

LIVING THE ADVENTURE

"You can't cross the sea merely by standing and staring at the water."
— Rabindranath Tagore

We all sat in a circle, young and old, as the scent of burning white sage drifted through the air. A medicine man was shaking his rattle and chanting some far off tune as a willow peace pipe, long as an arm, was solemnly passed from hand to hand. I shivered a little in the cold, but not because I was on a mountaintop in Nevada. I shivered because the air-conditioning was set too high in the suburban Austin home where I sat with family and friends.

This was our "adventure."

Now, my friend who celebrated her 40th birthday by climbing Mount Kilimanjaro would argue hers was an "Adventure" with a capital "A." She's probably right. But having a family, jobs to juggle and not quite the energy I had in my youth, I'm grateful for all the lowercase adventures I can get. After all, I don't want to end up like Cayce.

Our dog Cayce would spend her days in the yard going from water dish to back door, favorite resting spot to swimming pool. These paths were so well used that the grass had died along her usual routes. The map of her life crisscrossed our yard in brown trails as she took the most efficient route, rarely getting off the beaten path.

I too have my trails, from house to school, grocery store to gym, favorite café to park. What I need now is less time on the trail, and more on the detour. I need to get off the deadening highway and onto the quirky side roads where novelty blooms.

I've decided that adventuring is a muscle like any other, and if not used, it atrophies. We constantly have a choice whether to use it or not. Shall we eat in the same restaurant tonight near the house, or explore a authentic diner tucked away on a street hung with piñatas on the other side of town? See a movie with our spouse, eating popcorn and oblivious to each other, or rent a canoe and listen to the crickets while paddling at dusk? Walk through the neighborhood, or skip?

It's a state of mind that looks for ways to stir things up a bit, shaking us out of our trance to pay attention and live more intensely. We open to not knowing how a situation will turn out. Our pulse quickens. We delight in the new.

This summer, I've been actively trying to get my adventure muscle back in shape. My 13-year-old daughter and I had a "body connecting" adventure by going to NiaSpace and dancing all night after drumming in a room full of joyous, noisy percussionists. My husband and I strolled South Congress on a Thursday night, a "texture" adventure where our senses lit up like the funky neon store lights as we listened to the grind of grunge music, watched purple Mohawks menace by and inhaled smells of steaming hot-dogs and motorcycle exhaust. Our adventures have been "artsy" at a Hawaiian Pirate Pajama Party that culminated in firing raku pottery at midnight, and more "entertaining" as we watched belly dancers jangle gold coins across their hips as hundreds of birds swooped overhead on Town Lake. It doesn't matter if your idea of a lowercase adventure is inviting a neighbor you barely know over for dinner or parachuting after work — the point is to do whatever is a stretch for you.

For my friend Shelby, belonging to an Adventure Club nudges her into doing what she otherwise might not. Every month, one of the 10 couples in the club plans an adventure, from laser tag to rock climbing to a martini and cigar party where everyone brings different martini ingredients. Bonds are forged as everyone steps out into new experiences together.

I think as we age, it becomes too easy to get smaller, spurred to action only by the gunfire of our to-do list. But when we're 80, will we remember the flowers given to us by a Hawaiian woman at a roadside stand, or our twice annual teeth cleaning?

It's not so much what you do as how open your mind is for exploration. It's about putting ourselves in mental and physical places that challenge us, titillate us, move us. The night my family and I participated in the Native American pipe ceremony, what we really shared was a mutual willingness to try something new, to step outside our day-to-day routines and into a strange land... even if it was only as far away as a suburban living room.

Discover Your Own Pearls

What were your last few adventures? Do you find yourself more drawn to "texture" adventures where you use all your senses, or to mental or spiritual ones? What's the common theme? If you don't feel there's enough adventure in your life, what's holding you back? Time? Creativity? Come up with something easy — say, checking out a new restaurant — and just begin...

WHAT WE RESIST, PERSISTS

"When you can soak up every single moment just as it is,
without needing or expecting it to be different,
then you've opened all the way."
— Raphael Cushnir

It all started with an overdue library book that fell behind the bed. Our family was heading out the door for a fall festival, excited about picking pumpkins in the brisk fall sunshine. Since the library was en route, we decided to rescue the wayward book before we left. For a family ready to get out the door, that was the wrong move.

It sounded so easy — except for the fact that we have a wooden platform bed connected to a headboard and nightstands. So, the operation entailed one person wedging a dolly under the bed/headboard combo and lifting 300 pounds while the other wildly ran a backscratcher under the bed in hopes of hooking the book and dragging it out. After 20 minutes of thwarted attempts, I finally stormed off in frustration.

As I sat glowering, I realized that once again I had been holding my breath. You know, that thing we do when we have a certain plan in play — in this case, get out the door and frolic in the fall sunshine — and something gets in the way. So, instead of accepting it and flowing with the changes, we resist. We turn into stone. We judge the situation as bad, slap a label on it and try to get rid of it. Quickly.

The irony is that the more we close off to the situation, the worse it gets. We're not only mad (or sad, or frustrated...), but we're mad about being mad, which intensifies it.

Once I realized what I was doing, I took a deep breath as I recalled a line by Henry Miller, "Everything we shut our eyes to, everything we run away from, everything we deny, denigrate or despise, serves to defeat us in the end. What seems nasty, painful, evil, can become a source of beauty, joy and strength, if faced with an open mind."

An open mind, huh? Seemed like a stretch, but I gave it a try. I decided to accept everything, including my frustration. Once I looked head-on at my feelings and acknowledged them, suddenly they began to soften, grow legs and purr. When I returned to the bedroom and we lifted the bed again, this time it came crashing down on a pen, splattering ink all over the floor and my legs. My panic stricken husband thought it was blood. But instead of screaming, I laughed. My reaction might not have been a miracle of epic proportions, but it was a miracle nevertheless.

All day long we're faced with feelings or events that we instinctually resist. We're stuck at a red light and grow impatient. Our telephone bill is screwed up so we call the company in anger. We get sick and feel sorry for ourselves. All those are opportunities to hold our breath, shut out life and look away in distaste. Or, to open to it and accept with compassion right where we are at that moment.

Last night I went to get groceries during my youngest daughter's gymnastics class. My older daughter was home alone and an electrician was on the way over. I was trying to quickly pay for 9 bags of groceries when suddenly my credit card went on vacation. "Declined," the grocery clerk said. I swiped again. Declined. I looked at my watch — I was already five minutes late picking up my daughter. Swiped again. Declined. I could feel the embarrassment start to mount. The line grew longer behind me, people were staring. "It's always worked before," I mumbled weakly. I didn't even have any checks with me, as I'd written my last one for gymnastics tuition an hour ago. Now panic was setting in. The frozen chicken thawed as my cheeks heated up.

Then, I realized what I was doing. Resisting... again. After all, this hadn't been scripted in my perfect day scenario. So, while part of me was in the middle of the mess, another part began calmly, even compassionately, observing. It stated the obvious — here was a mother in a grocery store, embarrassed and worried about being late to get to her daughters. Perfectly normal reaction. I accepted it, which amazingly gave the whole situation some breathing room. It's as if you have a temperamental child, and instead of scolding her, you hug her, opening a space for transformation.

By the time I was back in the car, 15 minutes late to get my daughter and with the groceries still sitting at the store, I could feel the fall air through the window and appreciate its soft bite. Intense embarrassment had mellowed to inconvenience. I felt a flicker of pleasure at the moon rising in my rear view window. When I picked up my daughter and told her the story, she showered me with little kisses and a giggle when I said I imagined myself mopping the produce aisle to pay for the groceries. Back at HEB, the ice cream was melting; here in the car, my resistance was, too.

Discover Your Own Pearls

Next time an emotion begins to arise — anger, sadness, frustration, envy — try to observe it passing through you. See where it turns up in your body (headache, backache, clenched fists...) and what it feels like. Don't judge your emotion (I shouldn't be so annoyed at my son!), just observe and let it be. As you compassionately watch it, it will change. The edge comes off and you begin to see that it's not a block wall, but something that shifts and eventually disappears...

THE PERFECT VACATION

"I do not really like vacations. I much prefer an occasional day off when I do not feel like working. When I am confronted with a whole week in which I have nothing to do but enjoy myself, I do not know where to begin. To me, enjoyment comes fleetingly and unheralded; I cannot determinedly enjoy myself for a whole week at a time."
— Robertson Davies

"Just one more day," I thought as I walked through our neighborhood in 93 degree heat, a garbage truck noisily belching past me, a mosquito lighting on my arm just as I hopped off the sidewalk to avoid a skateboarder. Just 24 hours until vacation. Then, hello cool mountain air and skies so vast they'll evaporate my cares. Our family was headed for "The Land of Enchantment," and I was ready to be enchanted.

A week later I was set squarely in paradise, hiking a pine-needle strewn trail as the sun set, and thinking blissful thoughts like... had I remembered to turn off the thermostat before we left town? Perhaps those eggs this morning had gone bad, because my stomach feels kinda weird. Which of course led to, I wonder how much longer this trail will last?

Huh? We paid dearly in air fares, accommodations and car rental fees for... this?

Somehow I had thought that by taking a "vacation," defined on dictionary. com as a "period of time devoted to pleasure, rest or relaxation," that I'd find exactly that. I wasn't naïve enough to expect pleasure to wash over me sun-up to sun-down. But I had at least expected my happiness quotient

215

to rise significantly. I thought there'd be some sort of mathematical equation — say, X dollars out of my bank account = X amount of joy in my system? Or perhaps one degree increase in happiness for every degree decrease in heat?

But no, what I realized was that I reached the same level of happiness on vacation as I did at home. Luckily, my level of happiness is relatively high. Yet, I found the things that tripped me up in Texas also did in New Mexico. Impatience in a grocery store line at home meant impatience in the souvenir stand line on vacation. Moods that rise with sunlight and fall with the rains at home did the same on the road.

Of course, I figured I was the exception. Everyone else was able to drop their egos at the luggage carousel and go merrily go on their way, explaining why I hear nothing but superlatives when others talk about their trips.

On the way home, however, I discovered something. We missed a flight connection in Dallas and had to kill a couple of hours at the airport, where I found a small book titled "The Art of Travel" in the newsstand. At one point, author Alain de Botton says of his trip to idyllic Barbados, "I was to discover an unexpected continuity between the melancholic self I had been at home and the person I was to be on the island…"

Bingo. At least on the continuity part.

He went on to say that unlike the continuous, enduring contentment that we anticipate before we travel, our actual happiness with a place rarely endures for longer than ten minutes at a time. He adds, "New patterns of anxiety inevitably form on the horizon of consciousness, like the weather fronts that mass themselves every few days off the western coasts of Ireland."

Aha! He didn't experience nonstop bliss, either. Joy comes in snatches, not days. While I didn't find whole afternoons of peak experiences on my trip, I did find moments of joy scattered like wild flowers. I'll never forget riding the ski-lift down the mountain into an expanse of clouds, or seeing my daughter light up in a brand new red cowboy hat, or the sweet smell of desert creosote after a fast, hard rain in Albuquerque.

But I have joyful moments every day at home, too. Which leads to the question, why travel?

That was exactly the question that dogged Xavier de Maistre in 1790. He, in fact, wrote a book called "Journey Around My Bedroom" where he "rediscovered" his surroundings by changing into pink and blue pajamas and then traveling to his bed. Looking at it with fresh eyes, he took immense pleasure in the fact that his sheets matched his pajamas, and he felt grateful for the nights he had spent in its embrace.

He felt that one doesn't have to travel far distances to deeply "see" what's around them. Perhaps that's the starting point — learning to appreciate what's around you, which translates into living more deeply at home and thus vacationing more deeply. If he could travel around his bedroom and find a vista of new things, couldn't we perhaps spend some time looking with fresh eyes upon our own surroundings?

I think about that now that I'm back in the heat, walking. But this time, as I follow the asphalt trail, I stop to rub the sweaty necks of the horses I pass, noticing their fat tongues rhythmically caressing a salt lick. I observe the dark shade of late summer leaves. And I feel bliss. Right in my own backyard...

Discover Your Own Pearls

Remember some peak experiences you had on your last vacation and try to recreate those at home. If, for instance, you found a funky little shop and had a good chat with the owner because you were in a state of vacation "fascination," why not find a new shop in your neighborhood and see what you can find of interest there? Talk to the owner and find something interesting about her. Be open for a new and different experience, and you just might have one!

ONCE YOU LEARN TO RIDE

*"For something has happened
To your youthful passions,*

*That great fuel
You once had to defend yourself
Against becoming tamed.*

*And your eyes now often tell me
That your once vital talent to extract joy
From the air
Has fallen into a sleep."*
— Hafiz

I was driving to meet my friend Peggy for lunch when she called to say her car had broken down. I made some consoling noises, and then started looking for an exit so I could head back home as we rescheduled lunch. Then she added, "So, I'll be 15 minutes late — I'll just pop on my bike and ride to the restaurant."

Huh?

Now, I know that someone planning to ride a bike isn't strange. But, frankly, 90 percent of the people I know who ride bikes are much shorter than me. After all, that's something kids do, wearing shiny thunderbolt helmets and ringing bells on the handlebars while they're whizzing over to a friend's house a block away for milk and cookies. Adults rarely do it; when they do, it's just because the health club is closed. They put on spandex bicycling outfits, then ride a well-known, traffic-free path to get their heart optimally pumping before coasting home.

Not Peggy. Although well into middle age, that day she hopped on her bicycle and wheeled up to the restaurant 15 minutes later, dressed not in spandex but a beautiful black shell accentuated by chunky ethnic jewelry.

I couldn't help but be amazed. I asked her if she had always seen the bike as an effortless second choice in situations such as this? (Personally, I wouldn't have thought of it in a hundred years.) No, she answered. It was all part of reconnecting with her past.

She went on to explain that at one point in her life, she simply wasn't feeling as much joy as she wanted to. So, with the help of a life coach, she mentally went back into her childhood and looked for things that made her happy, things worth pulling forward into adulthood. The bicycle (she couldn't live without "wheels" as a kid) made the cut. Before long, she was riding again.

How interesting, I thought. I suddenly felt very stodgy sitting there, my car in the parking lot and my grown up ruts surrounding me. Why couldn't I pop on a bike to get to a lunch date, too, I wondered (other than the fact that my life would be in peril from daydreaming in the midst of Austin traffic)?

I started thinking about the types of things that brought me joy as a kid — walking on stilts, riding horses, putting on plays and catching fireflies. Hobbies weren't all I'd left behind. There were also mind-states and natural ways of being. As a child I had reveled in nature, often sitting and writing poetry in my side yard, my pen scratching on paper as the leaves rustled and my schnauzer padded across the grass. Life seemed limitless, expansive.

My husband, who always worked with his hands building something or another as a kid, had stopped doing that as an adult. Then, a few years ago, the passion struck again and he turned to sculpting with his hands. He couldn't get enough of it.

When my 15-year-old daughter was younger, she used to

love swinging in the back yard after school, singing as she flew through the air. That, too, has stopped.

It's as if at some point in the transition from child to adult, someone makes a comment or culture pushes its views on us ("this is silly kid's stuff") and we let go of the simple things that feed our souls. We close a door. My friend Peggy simply walked back through the door, spotted the bicycle and wheeled it back out.

As we talked, I thought about the poetry books lining my bookshelves and the beckoning expanse of grass in our back yard. I contemplated the little girl theatrically doing plays in her spare time. I think I'll pay her a visit...

Discover Your Own Pearls

Take a few moments, close your eyes, and remember back to your childhood. What gave you joy? What hobbies did you have? What made you feel lighthearted? Just be there for a few minutes... Then, see if there's anything worthwhile from your past that you can bring into your life now. Take one small step.

LOW-TECH CONFESSIONS

"If you want to be free, learn to live simply.
Use what you have and be content where you are."
— J. Heider

D o you ever have nightmares where you strut to school, only to realize you have no clothes on? I do. I also dream that I'm frantically running around the house and all the household equipment has rebelled against me. Like a science-fiction fantasy, I can't run the alarm clocks or DVD players, the camera won't give me its pictures, and the computer scoffs at me before disconnecting from the internet. Then I yawn, stretch and remember — that's not a dream, it's my life...

Somehow amid the mad technology rush of the last 20 years, I got left behind. Were I not married to a technology devotee, who knows where I'd be. Probably plunking out stories on my high-school Smith-Corona typewriter and watching one channel on a black and white TV. But to both my joy and frustration, my husband has tried pulling me into modern times. All the latest gadgets nest in our home. But as they say, you can lead a horse to water, but you can't make her program the DVD player...

When left alone with the DVD player, I eye it as a wrestler does her opponent. Who will win is anybody's guess. I start with laying out the four remotes that control the various technology systems connected with the television, and then start a highly organized assault of button pushing. Sometimes the movie I want pops up and I raise my arms in victory. Other days, a smirking blue screen stares back at me.

If I admit defeat on a late-night flick and go to bed, another challenge awaits. The alarm clock. This Sharper Image model has buttons, things that slide, and switches that click on and off, all the while offering up soothing sounds to help offset the mounting frustration I feel when I set the alarm for 6:30 a.m. and it goes off at 2 a.m. That's usually when I grab the old analog clock off our mantle and switch the alarm to "on." Since there's only one button, you can do it in the dark. Pure simplicity.

To make it worse, I'm surrounded by the technically facile — my husband, my children, my siblings and all the neighborhood high-tech employees. After hearing about some of my technological lapses, a few neighbors show nothing less than shock. I've lost my 21st century merit badge, my admittance to civilized culture. If I can't retrieve the messages on my cell phone, why, what next? Will they find me taping strings between styrofoam cups and trying to call them? I must say, though, that they don't realize the whole story. After all, I'm very good at turning on the microwave oven and Jacuzzi tub...

Perhaps, I dream, I'll just check out and spend my time picking daisies and taking pictures of clouds. And then I remember — I can't work the digital camera, either. Or, to clarify so you don't imagine I'm completely inept, I can take photos... assuming I don't accidentally bump into something. At that point, an unknown blinking light comes on along with a few unintelligible symbols in the viewfinder, and I'm paralyzed as to how to make sense of it — a feeling akin to being dropped in downtown Tokyo without a translator.

But lately, the amazingly simple revelation has come to me that if I really wanted to master the megabyte, I would have. I realized with relief that I'm not a deficient human being who can't work the wireless web — I'm one who has prioritized. What Plato said ages ago rings true for me. "In order to seek one's own direction," he said, "One must simplify the mechanics of ordinary, everyday life." Were I to focus on the equipment around me, I'd lose myself. It's my low-tech orientation that feels right to me — as right as a mouse in hand for others.

My talents lay not in fixing computer viruses, but in rocking my daughter as she struggles through a cold virus. I can't decipher my cell phone, but I can decipher my husband's needs before he even expresses them. I set a table with love and draw my family around it, but I can't for the life of me set my digital watch. And sometimes, I'd rather put down the digital camera and jump into a pile of leaves with my dog than capture it through the viewfinder.

Don't get me wrong — I'm appreciative of the high-tech conveniences and admire those who master them, and those who help me with them. What would I do without my e-mail? But I like the feel of simple living, with a few high-tech goodies thrown in to enhance rather than distract from what's important.

Sometimes I dream that all the household equipment has rebelled against me. That's when I smile and walk outside, leaving remote and mouse behind, and entertain myself watching old-fashioned clouds float by.

Discover Your Own Pearls

Are you running your technology or is your technology running you? Make conscious decisions. Is it worth having a certain piece of technology if you spend half your time fixing it? Or don't know how to work it? Bring each thing into your home with thought and care, and keep it only if it simplifies or adds to your life...

ALL I WANT IS... EVERYTHING

*"Instead of wrestling toward what you are convinced ought to be
going on, it might be refreshing to approach events without armor,
meeting their nakedness with your own nakedness."*
— John Tarrant

The sky was clear and we all took off in the best of spirits. Humming songs, reading books, doing Sudoku puzzles on the plane, our family of four was headed for a vacation in Sedona.

There was nothing marring the picture. Who could argue that a week in paradise visiting family and friends would be anything but ideal?

So that's why I found myself scratching my head and wondering just what happened that morning. Here we were, with beautiful weather and gorgeous mountains just outside the condominium window... feeling miserable.

Part of it, I groused to myself, was the inflatable beds some of us had slept on. Also, we had forgotten to pick up ingredients to cook breakfast and everyone was circling the one leftover muffin like vultures. Finally, some of us wanted to hike, some preferred shopping, while another wanted to laze around the condo all morning reading books. We had to compromise.

As I was sitting in a beanbag chair by the picture window, wishing that all sorts of things would be different — the breakfast, the moods of my family, the indoor temperature — I picked up a book. A little escapism was in order and there was no chocolate around.

As sometimes happens, the first passage I opened to was almost embarrassingly directed right at me. In the book "Trust in Mind," author Mu Soeng wrote that often what makes us unhappy is our "obsession with trying to fix the world around us according to our preferences."

Hmmmm... obsession with trying to fix the world around us? These weren't obsessions, my mind retorted. Just because I wanted a few things to be tweaked somewhat? All I asked for was a hike by 9 a.m. so that we'd have time to sightsee — plus a firmer bed, a warmer room, no snoring, and that everyone around me was cheerful... I slunk further down into my chair as I continued reading. Soeng wrote, "...we find we are essentially trapped in a world of reactivity, pulled this way and that in response to what we like or don't like."

I imagined a ping pong ball bouncing around Sedona — with my face on it.

What was keeping me from having a good time that morning wasn't the location or my family, but my own long list of preferences about how things "should" be.

I remembered the hike the day before. My preference was to climb the side of the mountain in the sun. We started off in a direction that we thought might accomplish that goal, but started grousing almost immediately: It's too cold. This doesn't have the incline we want. Where is this trail going, anyway?

We were being swatted around by our addiction to having our preferences met.

What's wrong with preferences, you might wonder? After all, there's no crime in preferring strawberry ice cream to vanilla, or tea over coffee.

But what I discovered was that it's not preferences that get us in trouble; it's when we subconsciously add the words, "and I won't be happy until I get things my way."

If all they have is vanilla, do we accept and move on, or throw a tantrum? Do we inwardly complain and rebel, amplifying it, or do we simply register the disappointment and let it be? Are we addicted to our way, or able to go with the flow?

And that's the lesson of vacations. When we're at home, we arrange things the way we want them — the furniture, the type of car we drive, the route to work.

On vacation, we're forging new territory every moment as we adjust to unfamiliar rental cars, new beds, different people. So, expecting everything to line up just as we want it is even more of a stretch. Yet we head out the door expecting bliss and are surprised when we come up short.

Sitting by the window, I started realizing how many of my preferences were silly things that I could easily let go of. So what if I was chilly, I thought? I'd put on a sweater.

I also saw which ones I couldn't control and needed to accept.

I couldn't change my bleary eyed husband, who was cranky from a bad night's sleep. But I decided I had enough compassion in that moment to let him be. I also suggested a morning activity, but agreed that any of the final choices was OK with me. After all, the beauty of the surroundings and being with my family was enough – everything else was icing.

As I changed my perspective, the atmosphere seemed to change, growing more peaceful.

With each breath, I could feel my tight grip on all my "wants" loosening. I looked out at the mountains and instead of looming, they were now ripe with possibility.

Nothing had changed — there were just fewer preferences coming between me and my paradise.

Discover Your Own Pearls

Notice when you have strong feelings about wanting something to be different, whether it's that the cushion on your chair be softer or the weather warmer. What can you control, what can you let go of?

WHEN THE CAT'S AWAY

"Man cannot live on chocolate alone; but woman sure can."
— Anonymous

I used to feel sorry for them. My friends would tell me their husbands were leaving on a business trip, and I'd imagine the wives like those in old movies, mournfully waving their kerchiefs as the car drove out of sight.

But now I know better. They boohoo for about five minutes — and then break out the Godiva chocolates. After all, when the cat's away, the mice get... self-indulgent.

It wasn't until a couple of weeks ago, when my husband left for a weekend at a fraternity reunion, that I truly understood this mindset. After he left, my 14-year-old daughter and I looked at each other uncertainly and then, almost at the same time, said "chick flick!" We snagged a copy of "Must Love Dogs," threw in a pint of Ben and Jerry's ice-cream and swung by the nearby Greek restaurant for pastitsio and gyros, the comfort foods of my youth.

I hate to admit it — after all, I love my husband in a big, soulmate-ish, 'till-death-do-us-part kind of way — but I was actually excited. Marriage is about many wonderful things, but one downside is compromise. This weekend, my inner toddler wanted it to be about me, me, me... okay, and the kids, too.

Late that night, I plopped into bed with a pile of books beside me. No one complained. I read, and no one suggested we turn out the lights. In fact, when I finally slept, no one snored, bounced or pulled the covers. I was a princess upon my mattress with no pesky peas or husbands to interrupt my beauty sleep. The next morning I slept as the sun rose, without the noise of coffee brewing or dog leashes jangling for imminent walks. Selfish bliss.

As I lay in bed, I realized how rare it was that I indulged myself. Part of my psyche always seemed to be focused on taking care of others' needs, harmonizing the home environment, solving problems. But this break felt good.

Later that day, I picked up the phone and called a friend. Just what was it like when her husband left home, I asked? I heard a pause, then a chuckle and she asked, "The truth?" Well… yes. It's fabulous, she answered. My kids and I eat cereal and milk every night for dinner and I don't do the dishes.

Now I was really intrigued and started talking to more friends. The confessions came pouring out. My husband's the disciplinarian, said one, so when he's gone I let the kids jump on the bed. Another is joined in bed by her dog and her daughter. Yet another takes the first opportunity to go to a pricey nearby deli, buying delicacies he normally poo poos spending money on.

It's as if, when the husbands leave, women who have been compromising and carefully shaping their lives give it a rest. The seams of responsible living let loose.

Cooking and housekeeping are the first to go. Bachelorette eating could mean anything from macaroni and cheese every night to desserts for dinner. Or eating every night at a restaurant they love and their husbands hate. Often toys stay on the floor and make-up sprawls on the counter. Outdoor dogs come in; floor-only dogs lounge on the sofas.

As one friend explained, as a stay-at-home mother she subconsciously feels like she's married to the "boss." And when the boss is gone, the labor slacks off. Big time. Wanna stay in pajamas all day? No problem. Wanna get a big, messy art project and spend hours playing with paint, then leave the brushes out to get dry and cracked? No one will lecture.

The lines crossed are different for everyone. One woman's revolt is an unmade bed. Another becomes a completely different person, the slovenly shadow of her prompt, prim everyday exterior. It's like teenage rebellion.

No one would want to live like this all the time. You can savor one chocolate, but a whole box would make you sick. So, after a couple of days, we welcome our husbands back. One woman says that his frequent trips are the reason that their marriage has stayed so healthy and strong for 20 years. As much as she loves him, his presence is another demand in her life and a few days of pure, uncomplicated "me-time" is her recipe for happiness.

Granted, being home alone with very young children or having a husband who constantly travels is no recipe for relaxation. Neither are those times when the kids are up all night with the flu or the water heater line breaks and floods the house, as it did to me one husband-free weekend.

As women, we've learned the finer points of care giving, sacrifice and compromise. Perhaps it's time to give more attention to the art of "me, too." Especially when it includes Godiva chocolates.

Discover Your Own Pearls

Is there a part of you that is sometimes repressed when your spouse is home? What part is that? How can you either get more time for yourself to express that aspect or integrate that part of you into your relationship?

TO E-MAIL OR CALL

"This 'telephone' has too many shortcomings
to be seriously considered as a means of communication.
The device is inherently of no value to us."
— Western Union internal memo, 1876

When my cell phone rings, it's always something of a shock to me. It's not that my concentration comparing peaches in the grocery store produce aisle has been absurdly interrupted by the Mexican Hat Dance. It's more that a minor miracle has just occurred. Someone found me.

This is statistically improbable for a number of reasons. Half the time I forget my phone in the car. Or forget to charge the batteries, or to turn the ringer on. I might even have it in my purse in good working order, but between the first ring and my ability to burrow to the bottom of my bag, past tissues, broken barrettes and an old school play program, the exasperated caller has hung up. Sometimes they leave a message. I don't know how to retrieve those, either…

Now, I can already see your condescending lifted brow, hear your cluck cluck of disapproval at my cell phone carelessness. You've got a smug smile because you, of course, always have your phone turned on, charged up and within easy reach. In fact, you probably also know how to instant message on it and take snapshots of friends. Good for you.

You've scored an "A" on cell phone smarts, but what about e-mail? Admit it — you think checking the inbox every leap year is sufficient. I'm on to you.

When it comes to high-tech communicating between friends, everyone has their preferences. Sure, we'd all love unlimited time chatting over pecan-crusted chicken salads at swank eateries, but short of that we have to rely on technology to keep friendships going, often by e-mail or cell phone. But when it comes to picking preferences, people's passions can be pricklier than a peck of pickled peppers. Some e-mailers I know guiltily admit that when a phone rings, they'd rather clear the refrigerator of last week's moldy leftovers than answer it. Phone users admit they so abhor e-mail, they've resorted to "losing" messages in order to avoid answering them. Once in our comfort zones, we don't want to be moved.

Personally, I'm an e-mail aficionado. I love to clatter amidst words, sending irreverent thoughts through cyberspace one moment, practical missives the next. E-mails arrive with a cheery ding, efficiently landing in my inbox, surprising me with everything from hale greetings to tepid news.

On the other hand, if I answer the cell phone while I'm driving, given my already dangerous proclivity to daydream, I'm likely to finish the conversation on top of a telephone pole. When the phone rings at home, it seems slightly ridiculous to shoot out of the shower, wet hair clinging spaghetti-style around my head, and dash past open windows just to pick up the receiver and hear about how I need an alarm system for my home — presumably so thieves won't catch me running naked for the phone. To me, a ringing phone isn't so much an immediate call to action as an option to be pondered. But hey, at least I ponder. Some people told me they NEVER answer the phone — why else were answering machines invented, they reason?

"Phone calls require me to respond immediately or risk sounding harried and uninterested, depending on what I'm doing when someone calls. However, e-mail allows me to take the time to respond with full attention... when I choose and according to my time schedule," says Jennifer, a working mom.

On the other hand, phones offer immediacy, laughter and inflection. And for those who like to multi-task, phones are ideal — often conversations are accompanied by the clanking of dishes, the roar of a dryer starting up, the crackle of cracker packages being opened for a hungry child. People on cell phones catch quick conversations on the fly. One friend uses her phone to complain to friends while sitting in traffic, alert them to clothing sales while in the mall, and pass the time waiting at the doctor's office.

A few people don't like either option. A school mom I know likes neither her mobile phone (cellular radiation) nor her e-mail (too much spam). Instead, she buys handmade paper and writes letters to friends.

Ah, the old days of handwritten communication. Now that I think about it, I do remember the texture of thick envelopes, pages stuffed with curlicue stories and ink-slanted tales. The slightly musty scent of the paper. The scrape of ball point.

I had forgotten the pleasure of writing and receiving letters because my vision had narrowed to the size of a computer screen. I realized I have been stuck without even knowing it. The mindless comfort of habit has replaced the freedom to experiment.

So perhaps this week I'll pick up a fancy box of stationary and actually find a pen that works. I'll charge up my cell phone. And when I'm sitting at one of Austin's infamously long red lights, I'll call one of my cell fiend friends and shock them out of their reverie... and quite possibly mine, too.

Discover Your Own Pearls

Do you prefer to use phones, e-mail or some other way of communicating with friends between visits? Have your tech preferences ever hurt friendships? Do you have mild preferences or strong feelings about one method verses another? Do you find yourself ever using that method out of habit or fear, rather than because it's the best way to reach out to someone in a particular moment? Why don't you try using a different method and see what happens?

DON'T PUT OFF UNTIL TOMORROW

"You don't have to see the whole staircase, just take the first step."
— Martin Luther King, Jr.

I've been meaning to start this column all day, but one thing or another got in the way. The unseasonably mild weather was too beautiful to pass up a hike. I had to order a computer part via telephone, and how was I to know I'd be put on hold for 18 minutes? Once I finally settled in my chair to write, darned if a chocolate craving didn't hit me right then, sending me into the kitchen where I noticed dishes that needed to be washed from last night's dinner.

Now that I'm finally writing, however, it strikes me as ironic that the subject I've been meaning to slay is... procrastination.

We all do it. At this very moment, my daughter is industriously peeling price stickers off gifts, instead of opening the daunting World History textbook next to her.

I know the feeling. Even as I pen this section, it flits in my head that my nails need filing and that I should respond — immediately — to the emails I got this morning. The reason I'm not giving into temptation — this time — is that I know the cost of a choice to procrastinate.

It feels good for a few moments, even giddy, and then the energy drain begins. Whenever I think about what I'm avoiding, a little more energy gets depleted. The longer I avoid it, the larger it becomes. Hours, days or months go by and suddenly, what was once a relatively simple project morphs into a fire-breathing dragon, a terrible beast staring me down.

Take my photo organizing project, for instance. When my husband and I got married 18 years ago, I meant to put our wedding photos in albums. When the kids were growing up, I really intended to organize all our images in books. When we went digital, I figured I'd print them out and perhaps even scrapbook some of them. By now, the beast has grown to 20 times its original size, so approaching it will take a big sword and stamina.

Yet with that sword, I can cut it down into smaller pieces. Organize one box one week, buy a few albums the next week. Once we break daunting tasks into smaller, more manageable bits, it feels like pulling the curtain aside to reveal the Wizard of Oz. Inside isn't something scary, just a man with a megaphone who has been filling our heads with scary thoughts. This is overwhelming! I'll never do it right! It must be avoided at all costs!

The thought of doing something perfectly also trips us up. That's how it is with my writing. The blank page leers at me, sputtering smoke and daring me to write something profound on it. That's when I sidestep it with my "bad writing" approach. I tell myself I just have to start with a page of bad writing. The worse the puns, the better. Dangling participles? No problem. The point is just to enter the dragon's lair for five minutes and start, imperfectly.

Other tasks appear more intimidating. We might avoid them because we simply feel too tired, too much like our day has been spent following "shoulds" rather than "wants." That can lead us straight into limbo-land. You know the place. You feel too drained to accomplish what you need to, but you feel so guilty about not tackling your to-do list that that you can't have fun doing anything else, either.

That's the time when perhaps we need a dip in the bubble bath rather than the dragon's lair. We just need to step aside and take care of ourselves, to rejuvenate for what's ahead.

After we've met our own needs, we may even enter the lair whistling a tune and do a dance with the dragon. It becomes downright fun. Once dreaded tasks are now dispatched with ease.

Right now, the only thing spewing fire is the blaze in the fireplace in front of me. My youngest daughter is curled up on the chair reading. I've simply observed and let go of all my urges to procrastinate, leaving me plenty of energy to write this article. I'm almost finished, and then perhaps I'll brew up a latte, open the card table, and start going through my boxes of photos...

Discover Your Own Pearls

Name one thing that you are procrastinating about. Perhaps you'd like to organize the bathroom closet and haven't done it. Or you need to confront someone and you're avoiding it. What toll does this avoidance take on you? Right now, look at your appointment book and set aside 20 minutes this week to move ahead — imperfectly — in this area.

POSTCARDS FROM HOME

"A woman's path need not always take her many miles from home. It will, however, always invite her to let go of where she's already been, and to be open to the Mystery of where she's going. Grace will be her guide and will ask her to trust in her own wisdom. In this way, a woman's path will invariably lead her back to her true self, and no path is ever more valuable than this."
— Sally Lowe Whitehead

L ook at this, I whined at my husband, shaking a beach-scene postcard from Australia. Everyone but us is off someplace glamorous on vacation, I grumbled. Yes, I had agreed that we'd forgo trips this summer, but I wasn't happy about it. As I dropped the postcard in the trash, I was feeling frumpy, frustrated and getting crankier by the minute.

To top it off, the next day summer camps started for my daughters. Both were on the same schedule, but opposite ends of town, meaning I'd have to puzzle out complicated carpooling strategies to get everyone there and back. As it ended up, the only solution was for me to drive downtown every morning, fighting rush hour traffic for half an hour before the 10 second drop-off. The salty sea air was sounding better and better…

The first morning of this schedule, I dragged out of bed and started getting ready for the commute. An e-mail popped up from a friend in Colorado. Oh, you should see the mountains, she oohed. I flipped off my computer.

After dropping the girls, I sat in the car, deciding what to do. I was only five minutes from the hike and bike trails that snake along Town Lake. It had been ages since I'd walked them, I realized, so despite the heat I headed over.

As I started walking, I noticed a nice breeze coming off the lake. A field of sunflowers stretched out before me. I ran into an old friend of my daughter's, newly arrived back from a semester in Hungary. The further I walked, the more I became energized. Every sense seemed to blink alive. I was soaking it all in – the carefree energy of splashing dogs, the salty sweat of runners, berries breaking red beneath my feet as I began to jog. Tomatoes ripened on the vine in a community garden I passed; a lawn chair beckoned weeders to sit and rest. I jogged past scents of soft summer leaves and sand dampened by wriggling fish pulled from the water.

The next day I was back, this time with my yellow dog. I went even further, spending an hour and a half along the trails. Afterwards, we sat alone on a dock watching the kayakers go by, slivers of red, blue and green dropping oval paddles into the water. My heart felt ripe and full. Through my body, I was reconnecting with something deep inside. Something vital.

Driving home, I left the windows open to cool off the dog. The din of the traffic sounded like the roar of the ocean, and we intrepidly swam through it.

The following week, I decided to dive into the city. Here, I found a sea of suits instead of spandex. As I walked, shopkeepers sprayed off their sidewalks, the water glistening with the newly hatched sun. A box of yellow and orange flowers was wheeled onto the pavement. A side alley beckoned. A thin veil of smoke rose, floating out from café back doors along with the smell of frying bacon. A man jumped out of a truck and disappeared through one of the doors with a box of artichokes artfully balanced on his shoulder.

As I explored, I thought of vacations I've taken where the mindset and stress of home seemed to come right along with me. Nothing was transformed. Other trips were pleasant diversions at best. The best moments were those when I was struck with wonder and delight, along with a deep sense of connection with everything around me. A feeling of "enough." In other words, how I felt at that moment.

I realized how often I had confused the desire to feel that certain way with the surety that it could only be found someplace else. Once I hit that Hawaiian beach, or the French café, I had assumed, this feeling would come and my money will have been well spent. I had forgotten that what's essential isn't how far we go, but that we open with curiosity to what's spread right before us.

This year, I didn't take a summer vacation — it took me. So when I pick out postcards to send to friends, I'll be looking for just the right message. Perhaps ones that say, "Greetings from Beautiful... Home."

Discover Your Own Pearls

How can you make tomorrow a "vacation?" Is there a part of town you can explore that you've never been to? What about going somewhere during a different time of day than you're used to — say, a local diner at 6 a.m. when the regulars are hanging out? Or a mountain at midnight? Try taking a walk ½ mile from your house instead of in your own neighborhood.

GOTTA GET IT

"What difference does it make how much you have?
What you do not have amounts to much more."
— Seneca

T here wasn't much reason or thought. I just knew I had to have it. But then again, I suppose that's the way most addictions work.

I somehow got in my head that we must have a game table. I had visions of my daughters' friends coming over and playing foosball and air hockey, pizza warming in the oven downstairs, music playing, an atmosphere of jovial camaraderie filling the house.

No matter that we have no space for such a table. No matter that I had already met my entertainment budget. No matter that my children hadn't expressed any desire for one. These were mere details.

One thing about compulsive buying, I've observed, is that there's always a sense of urgency involved. You don't just lollygag around and finally meander into a shop. Instead, it's a white hot, focused, intense energy oblivious to everything else. So, when I found my table in the paper — at a discounted price, no less! — I cajoled my husband to race off to get it, despite the fact that the girls were in a drama program starting in two hours. After all, I fretted, in two hours all the tables might be gone. Everyone else would realize what a bargain this was and rush the stores en masse. We had to hurry, hurry, hurry!

He arrived and picked up the table… sitting in an almost empty store amidst the dozens of other game tables that hadn't been sold.

You'd think that would be it — table bought, Mom happy. But no. A week later, I found another table with even more games in it, so I bought it. A few days later, when I spotted an ad for a game table with a black light — imagine slumber parties with the girls playing by the eerie glow of the black light! — I started heading to the car to buy it when I passed through the garage and saw the other two tables stacked up in boxes. That's when the absurdity of it hit me.

I had been blindly racing around town — Wylie E. Coyote in hot pursuit of the Roadrunner — searching for the perfect game table. But what I really wanted, I realized, was the perfect day. That Norman Rockwell idea of people playing and laughing, having fun, the warmth of friends and family gathered and enjoying life together. Since I had never taken the time to ponder why I wanted the game table, I didn't understand that the need driving it could be met in a hundred other, more creative, ways.

I remembered the year I had bought six wall calendars, thinking I "needed" all of them, and later realizing that those purchases were just reflecting the disorganization of my life at that time. My only need was to get organized, not get all those calendars. And when the kids were toddlers, I remember fantasizing about a set of lawn furniture I had seen. The picture included extra plump cushions and a small glass table, all ready for appetizers and cold drinks, surrounded by laughing couples. What did I need? Some pampered time to relax away from kids and with friends, not the patio set.

The trick is to figure out the real need before you reach for your pocket book. This maneuver is complicated by the fact that most emotion-driven purchases are done quickly. You almost know that if you don't do it fast, or on the spot, common sense will take over. Can't have THAT happen!

But the true inner gift you receive from slowing down is the chance to look at your life and see what is calling to you, then meet it in a much more deeply satisfying way. Instead of the Botox to feel young again, why not take classes that enliven you and bring out your inner spirit? Or skip the red Porsche and find freedom instead by loosening up a workaholic schedule?

As it ended up, I kept one of the game tables and the girls did invite friends over to play with it — for a week. It now sits in the garage, crammed between a Zen Garden from my simplicity-seeking days and a dusty exercise bike. I never seem to find the perfect day to use these neglected items. I do, however, find lots of perfect days — without spending a dime.

Discover Your Own Pearls

Look around at the items in your garage, closets and house. What do they say about what you were trying to find at one point in your life? Pick a couple of things that you recently bought and see what they may be trying to tell you. What is the underlying need? Find it — and meet it.

LOSING YOURSELF

"If you don't get lost, there's a chance you may never be found."
— Author Unknown

My husband tactfully calls me "directionally challenged." In plain English, I get lost a lot. Unless the sun is setting right in front of me, I couldn't tell you north from south, east from west. I head out with the best of intentions, and one wrong turn later, I'm on another side of town driving by discount piñatas and menudo specials.

Most would hate this affliction. And admittedly, when I'm supposed to be at a party in south Austin and am instead asking for directions in a grubby gas station with pin-up calendars, I'd agree. But what I've discovered is that when I know my way perfectly, too often I cease to look around me. My drive becomes about the destination, not the journey. Yet when lost, one can't help but to be "looking." And when looking, you never know what you'll find.

I've happened across some pretty swell parks this way, along with restaurants and a tiny place to take my watch for a new battery. I've discovered neighborhoods with wide front porches and streets crowded with dogs and baby joggers. Ten minutes were whiled away chatting with a woman selling fuzzy peaches from Johnson City, and another 10 wandering past Persian carpets when I stopped for directions. When I was a travel writer, getting lost produced some of my best stories.

In fact, there's a magazine out now called "Get Lost," and it's not about telling someone to bug off! It's about adventure, about savoring the journey wherever it may lead.

So often we're very sure of ourselves. We think we know where we're going, whether it's the directions to a dinner party or navigating how to save for retirement. But sometimes we have to lose our way before we can discover what's important. We plan to be a hard-charging trial lawyer, and then get lost and became a ceramicist instead. We plan to have one child, but adopt five and a parakeet instead. We plan the perfect life, but get lost and find the adventurous, rocky, wild one, instead.

In "The Power of Myth," Joseph Campbell says of this path, "It's uncertain, and you don't know where you are going. There is danger, adventure, things you've never beheld before." Yet if we're too afraid to get off the highway, we'll never taste those back-road adventures.

When you're rushing toward your destination and focused only on the bumper of the car in front of you — which of course you must pass — the arrival is all that matters. The satisfaction comes only when we pull up at the post office and drop off the envelope, or sit down at the conference table for a meeting. The 30 minutes in the car becomes "non-time," because we're too focused on the end to appreciate the middle. But when we're lost, we're present.

In fact, getting lost can be a whole art form of its own. Imagine, for instance, getting lost in the grocery store. This isn't where you wander the aisles in a daze looking for the chutney. It's where you're so blown away by the beauty of the mangoes that you literally lose track of time and place. Or visualize getting lost in a relationship. Instead of just looking for how someone matches up with your pre-conceived notions of them, you are open to really looking, finding amazement at all their little quirks, turns and windy roads.

Some people may choose the straight and narrow; but me, I'll continue off-roading without a map. I'd rather lose myself in the passion of the moment than find myself in a predictable rut by the side of the road.

Discover Your Own Pearls

When you have a little extra time this week, head out to an area you've never been and drive around until you're thoroughly lost. Be totally present and see what you observe. When you've had enough, pull out your map and figure out how to get home. But don't leave until you've found a "story" about your adventure, whether an imaginative foray into the life of the person in the odd purple house, or a description of your lunch at a tiny, offbeat café.

DANCING WITH QUESTIONS

"The important thing is not to stop questioning."
— Albert Einstein

We were having a candlelit dinner, plates of butter-slicked lobster beside us, when he popped the question. "So," he drawled, narrowing his eyes in an intense, interested manner, "Would you give up half of what you now own for a pill that would permanently change you so that one hour of sleep each day would fully refresh you?" Hmmm, I pondered. I felt the rush of excitement as the question swirled around me, along with visions of settling in with a novel at 2 a.m. and writing poetry at 4 a.m. The possibilities beckoned like lanterns in the night.

As we dined, my husband and I were gleefully tossing questions to each other from my tattered copy of "The Book of Questions." Some people get giddy over flowers and candy. For me, all you need to do is ask a really good question. I love to sink my teeth into them, flipping them in the air like dog bones. I two-step with them, contemplate them, warm my hands on them. Questions are the spice that makes life fun.

Now, there are questions and there are Questions. You know the first kind. So, do you think it's going to rain, you ask the person next to you, staring up at the gray sky as you sit in the bleachers waiting for the football game to begin? Those questions are necessary niceties to lubricate our social wheels. But the ones I love are ones that make me think, that launch me on a journey of self-discovery or open paths to intimacy with another.

I love to tango with open-ended questions that have no "right" answer, such as whether or not there's life on other planets. Ethical ones are like calisthenics, making sure my character is in good shape. If I could have a million dollars or cure cancer for 1,000 people, which would I choose? Then there are questions wearing overalls and bearing a shovel, and I use those to dig, a scoop at a time. Are you very close to your sister? Why not? What would your perfect sister look like? Of course, there are also the deep, dreamy questions that gaze with soulful eyes and ask one, succinct line. How are you, really?

Some people claim they just can't think of questions. My friend Sandi collects questions the way others collect stamps or butterflies. She keeps an eye out for the unusual ones, then jots them down and files them for later use, either to ponder herself or ask someone else. Our family has several books of questions as well as TableTalk cards, which we pull out to propel a conversation from homework to contemplating what three changes we'd make if we were president.

To me, someone asking questions is a person with spunk, with curiosity. They don't go around with an attitude that they know it all. Instead, they are like the child who asks why, who has a fierce desire to understand, to inhale, to plunge into the world and quench their curiosity. When they're in your family or you meet them at a party, you're in luck.

More often than not, though, when you go to a social gathering you're not trying to shield yourself from the barrage of too many questions. You're wondering if anyone will bother to ask even one. My husband and I have come home from get-togethers with wonderful stories about the people we've met, their passions and quirks. But we felt invisible because no one had reciprocated.

Imagine instead going to an event where colorful questions were tossed about like confetti. Where questions irreverent, thought provoking, mundane, heart-felt and laser-sharp were quaffed along with the Perrier. What would it be like if we all got over our fears of "offending" someone, of stepping outside the narrow bounds of social propriety, and risked a dangerous question?

Even further, what if we asked ourselves a dangerous question? Author Tony Robbins summed it up best when he said, "The quality of one's life is directly related to the quality of questions you ask yourself." Try waking up Monday morning and instead of asking "What the heck's on my to-do list?" ask "How can I give back today?" Or take a walk and contemplate, "In what ways have I allowed my life to become too small?" Let the questions take you deeper into the wonder of life. Let the questions stir awakenings and even deeper questions. Let the dance begin.

Discover Your Own Pearls

What are the questions in your life right now? Are they all basic — when can I find time to do taxes? Or are they big and thought provoking — what is the feel, sound and smell of happiness? If you're long on the first kind and short on the second, try to incorporate more of the "big" questions. Expand your life to fit the size of your biggest questions...

TO ERR IS HUMAN...

"Imagine how it might feel to suspend all your judging and instead to let each moment be just as it is, without attempting to evaluate it as "good" or "bad." This would be a true stillness, a true liberation"
— Jon Kabat-Zinn

A ll I needed to hear were two words — I'm sorry. Okay, maybe six — I'm sorry, I made a mistake.
I was talking to the dog groomer on the phone. Behind me, our Labradoodle careened through the room with a huge plastic cone around his head, accidentally knocking over bric-a-bracs and bumping into chairs. You see, I continued, his "sanitary shave" was too close and now he has a bloody scrape that will take weeks to heal. That means keeping an oversized cone on his head to keep him from chewing — another headache I don't need right now.

I paused, waiting for her response. I wasn't expecting her to offer up her first-born as compensation, but I at least thought those 6 words might be tucked in there somewhere.

They weren't. I think he had the problem before he even came in, she asserted. (Why didn't I see that? Our highly evolved dog must have nicked himself while shaving...) When I didn't say anything, she tried again. Sometimes this type of thing happens to lighter colored dogs. (Huh?) And then she charged that if we bathed him more often, this wouldn't have happened. (Does that mean the cut occurred because she was shaving him with one hand and holding her nose because of the stench with the other?)

It's amazing how far we'll go to avoid admitting we've made a mistake. Our rationalizations are creative; our excuses, illogical.

It's like when a child spills a glass of milk. Sometimes, they'll sheepishly admit they goofed up. More likely, they'll accuse you of giving them too slippery of a cup. Or of hurrying them along and thus "making" them spill it. Just like I "made" the groomer's razor slip. It's all your fault, not theirs.

So why do people go to such great lengths to cover up their mistakes?

I was in a seminar once with Austin psychologist T. Flint Sparks, and he made an interesting point. He said in Asia, when someone makes a mistake, they're more likely to say, "I made a mistake, I'm human." Here in the West, we're more likely to say, "I made a mistake, I'm bad."

We immediately judge ourselves. We feel the burn of shame that comes when something goes amiss and our rosy view of ourselves is threatened. While slippery excuses are coming from our mouths, the mind is busy flogging itself. We forget that we're worthwhile humans, no matter how many mistakes we make.

Yesterday, my daughter Chloe and I were frantically getting ready for her sister Alix's birthday party. The guests were arriving in 30 minutes and Chloe had been working on and off all day to prepare, even surprising me by completing tasks I hadn't assigned to her. I hadn't noticed, though, because I was so focused on ticking off my own birthday to-do list. Finally, she came to me quite upset, claiming she had been working hard all day and the least I could do was acknowledge it.

I was taken aback. My first instinct was to remind her that the least she could do was help with her sister's party because Alix would have done the same for her. Plus, no one had praised me for all the work I'd done. Anger and defensiveness started rising. But when I caught them and looked deeper, I realized she was right. I should have thanked her. I had spilled the milk, so to speak, and was about to blame it on her. That was far easier than getting angry at myself.

So, I took a breath and acknowledged to myself that I'm human, not "bad." I make mistakes... all the time. By not being caught in my own sweep of rationalizations and emotions, I was able to really hear and respond to her. Then she grabbed the crepe paper, I got the balloons, and it was behind us.

As for the groomer, she eventually offered to pay for a visit to the vet for our dog. She still didn't admit she had blundered. But she paid the bill. I suppose the pain of her self-judgment got in the way of an apology. My final four words to her were left unsaid as well — I understand, you're human.

Discover Your Own Pearls

For the next week or two, start catching your thoughts after you've made a mistake or done something you feel guilty about. Perhaps you spoke angrily at your child just as they were leaving for camp, or you forgot to pick up dinner on the way home. Watch how you judge yourself. Then remember — you're human, not bad — and see how that feels...

AT WHAT COST?

"We can tell our values by looking at our checkbook stubs."
— Gloria Steinem

E ver since I've known her, my friend Sheila Curran has been working on one novel or another. In between diapers, in between our daily conversations, she stole time to write. We dreamed of the day she'd publish her first novel; I promised I'd be there to toast her success.

A few years ago she and I both moved to different states, but the friendship continued. This past summer, the big event happened. Her novel, "Diana Lively is Falling Down," hit bookstores around the country. I kept promising I'd join her at one of the book parties, imagining sipping glasses of champagne, clapping as she stood in the limelight. There was nothing stopping me from hopping on a plane and keeping my promise.

Nothing, that is, except me.

I could say the reason I didn't dash out and join her was money. And in a way it was. Termites had managed to invade our house, leading to siding being ripped off and replaced, and then the whole house being repainted. My oldest daughter had just gotten braces and we'd bought a new air conditioning unit. So I was doing more than the usual amount of financial catastrophizing.

But the bottom line was that if my husband had an event that meant a lot to him, I'd have encouraged him to go. When my daughters are interested in summer classes, I find a way for them to go. Spending money on others wasn't a problem; spending it on myself was.

I come by this habit honestly. My mother always outfitted her children in good clothes, but she only bought outfits on sale for herself. At restaurants, we ordered what we wanted; she'd get a cup of coffee. Money for our higher education was first priority; she made do with what was left. I reaped the benefits from this largess, but I also reaped the "me last" frame of mind.

So when the offer came of a weekend of book parties in Phoenix with Sheila and other close friends, along with a chance to visit my wonderful Greek relatives — an irresistible mix almost too heady to pass up — I did just that. I passed it up.

"I'd love to go," I said, "but so many expenses have come up, I just can't make it." Perhaps I could make it up to her, I thought. I'd send her a $40 flower arrangement to show I was thinking about her. With almost surgical detachment, I decided this trip was something I couldn't "afford," and let it go.

Luckily, when we have one idea, sometimes the universe has another. Two weeks before Sheila was scheduled for her Phoenix book signing and parties, my daughter Alix had to drop out of a camp and we were to be refunded the money. Take it and go to Phoenix, Alix urged me. Then another friend in Phoenix called and said that, if I went, I could stay with her and use her car.

It was getting tempting. But… no.

Finally, I took my thick skull to check airfares again and, out of nowhere, the price had suddenly dropped by almost $100. Within five minutes I had the ticket.

It wasn't until then that I was flooded with how much I had wanted to go all along, and how chillingly easy it had been to set aside my needs. I hadn't let myself feel my desires, the easier to stuff them away.

So, I flew off to Phoenix and reconnected with people who really matter to me. I sat by the pool with my relatives, inhaling the scent of creosote after a monsoon. I returned to my favorite restaurants, always with a friend in tow. Then I proudly listened at the book signing while Sheila read from her fabulous novel — ironically about a woman who learns to value herself and honor her own needs.

I celebrated Sheila... and I celebrated myself.

Discover Your Own Pearls

How conscious are you about money choices? Do you always come last? Or first? What does your spending reflect about where your priorities are? Are you happy with that reflection? Sit lightly with these thoughts for a few minutes and see what comes up.

JOURNAL PLAY

*"When asked how to write a diary by those just beginning,
I generally respond: 'Write fast, write everything, include
everything, write from your feelings, write from
your body, accept whatever comes.'"*
— Tristine Rainer

Sometimes I bring it thunderclouds of frustration, scrawled lightning — quick in words that gust across the page until they dissipate. Other times I sidle over to it like a lover, whispering gardenia-scented promises. Sometimes I bring poetry, other times feelings raw and unkempt, certainly not fit for company or to read aloud under a starry sky.

My journal waits for me with open arms. It doesn't judge. It doesn't respond hysterically with, "What, you've done that AGAIN!" It doesn't tune out when I come near, closing its pages and reading the sports section instead. It offers me a space to go that's always there, on my timetable, in my hour of need or joy. It is unconditional.

This relationship started when I was very young with a small yellow diary, its tiny lock and key guarding immense secrets like that on page 28 — "Today my grandmother made tollhouse cookies and cute Bobby Tomasin played his accordion for me." As a teen the secrets became bolder, filled with heart wrenching passages that fainted and wailed in dramatic fashion. As a mother of young children I retreated, stattaco-style, to my pages between diaper changes and snack preparations. Often it lay unused.

Today, I find my time and interests colliding again as I steal away to it for that powerful alchemy that turns the base metals of our thoughts into the gold of self-knowledge. When I catch myself drifting uncomfortably through the day with anxiety, I turn to my journal and name all my fears, biting their edges like coins to see if they're real or not. Just the act of naming them, shining a light on their shadowy maneuvers, is often enough to send them floating on their way like so many clouds on a summer's day.

Other times I'm overwhelmed, sped up, pelted by a thousand thoughts that muddle and mystify. So I take respite in the blank, inviting whiteness of the page, dipping my pen into it like a baptism, confessing my confusion. I slow down. Clarity and peace return.

"Rather than standing outside problems and cursing them as enemies, the diary allows you to enter and explore them as personal mysteries containing messages of inner meaning in your life," says Tristine Rainer, author of The New Diary.

There are many ways to explore these mysteries, from fast, cathartic free-writing to slicks of descriptive passages; from practical lists to dialoging with aspects of yourself or others.

Whatever the form, it's really all about observing. Let's say we're full of anger. We can either become lost in our anger and let it control us, or we can step outside of it and observe, roll it around our mouths like a sweet or bitter wine, noticing the flavor and bite of it. When we journal we get inside the anger, yet we also get distance and control. Patterns appear, and eventually a path to an insight.

Sprigs of joy plucked from our lives also lie between the pages. When pages fill with blooming, abundant moments, they grow in our lives. A salty beach breeze flows into our book one day, the rapid pulse of the hummingbird the next. Each moment that we choose to appreciate and record deepens us and opens the way for more.

But ultimately it doesn't matter if what we record is joyful or sad, brilliant moon or flat, clear sky. Our thoughts are as changeable as the weather. What matters more is that we're curious enough to write. To look. To greet ourselves on the page… and off.

Discover Your Own Pearls

Experiment with different journaling techniques. You can write non-stop, just letting thoughts flow to see what's there (no judging allowed). Or, list all your fears, big and small. You can have a "dialogue" with an aspect of yourself you're struggling with, such as your anger or your "fat self." Even a quick snapshot of the dominant emotions of your day is valuable. Whatever style fits YOU is the right one.

THE FIRE WITHIN

"A quiet mind cureth all."
— Robert Burns

It wasn't the kind of moment one would equate with happiness. I was lying on the couch, staring up at the expanse of white ceiling, burning up with a fever. As I lay there, the refrigerator hummed in the late morning quiet. A distant leaf blower faintly coughed. A fly zipped across the room, buzzing against the windowpane before heading to greener pastures.

None of that surprised me. But as I lay there, I heard something unexpected. Something rare. The silence that surrounded me was... inside my own head.

Gone was the usual mental cacophony that resided there, like so many screeching birds in a forest. Gone were the usual string of judgments, worries, to-do lists and rehashing of old events. It was as if the fever had burned away all the usual mental garbage and left behind a refreshing drink of quiet — a deep peace that came from having nothing on my mind but a fly swooping by.

I've read about controlled fires before. Forest rangers set small, manageable fires to clear out the underbrush in a forest, ridding it of the accumulated leaves, twigs and dead vegetation. It's healthier for the forest. I imagine that my wise body had started this fevered blaze to clear out the underbrush of my busy, cluttered mind...

An hour later chills set in. I wander into a darkened room and sit on the floor by the red glow of a heating lamp and warm my toes. My dog trots in, mud ringing his mustache from his latest romp in the backyard, and we stare at each other. He makes sense to me. Nothing much on his mind, either. He lies down, I lie down, and we take naps.

When my husband comes home from work, he notices scratch marks the dog has made in past months on our beautiful wood floors. He wonders if we'll have to replace the floors, which he reminds me will cost a small fortune. His mind spins out in worry. The dog and I look at him. We don't understand why he's getting upset. That's trivial. He needs to clear out some underbrush, I think, before lying down and watching a spider cling to the ceiling.

The next day the fever is even higher. I get some soup and go outside. Sitting on the grass in a patch of sunlight, I spoon the bright orange squash soup into my mouth like a baby, watching the steam rise from the mug and drift into the silence. What's important in this moment isn't complex or hard to find. It's not lost in the traffic or hidden in a mindless sprint through the day. It's nourishing my body. Taking care of myself. At another time what's vital may be loving my child, or talking frankly with my husband. But in this moment, I can hear myself think. Nourishment, my mind says.

My friend Sharon knows this concept well. She's simplifying her life, burning out all that isn't essential with the flames of her passion to live. She's surviving breast cancer. The best way to defeat it, she feels, is by dropping thought patterns or friendships that are poisonous to her. Getting rid of the underbrush has cleared her vision so she now sees what remains. She's not searching anymore — what's important has been found. As she sits on her patio, mostly bald and still nauseous from the chemotherapy, she tells me something amazing. Because of this newfound clarity and simplicity, she's never been happier…

Every year we prune the crepe myrtle in our front yard, cutting it down to its essential, bare bones so it can eventually bloom more fully. Just like with the fires, some of the old has to die before renewal can begin.

I think about that sometimes, now that my fever has broken and life is speeding up again. Sometimes the underbrush of my thoughts gets too dense. I lose my way. At those times, I stop and put all my attention on something simple — gazing at a white ceiling, listening to squirrel chatter — and my mind clears. I can see right through the forest to the trees.

Discover Your Own Pearls

Don't wait to get sick before you take a sick day. Instead, find someplace quiet and lie down. Give yourself permission to let go of everything — deadlines, worries, to-do lists — for whatever time you need. Imagine that what's happening in your busy life is like a heavy suitcase that you choose to put down for awhile — 5 minutes, an hour — knowing you can pick it up again when you're done. Then just relax and stare gently at something in the room, breathing in, breathing out. Even when our bodies are physically well, our minds and spirits still need some quiet time and nourishment. Just for this moment, feed yourself...